Flying Radio

Cors

ARGUS BOOKS

Argus Books
Argus House
Boundary Way
Hemel Hempstead
Hertfordshire HP2 7ST
England

First published by Argus Books 1989

ISBN 0 85242 995 9

Phototypesetting by GCS, Leighton Buzzard
Printed and bound in Great Britain by
William Clowes Ltd, Beccles

Contents

Chapter 1
Introduction

THERE SEEMS to be a general misconception in the public mind which equates the engine, or motive power of an aircraft, with the control functions. When conversation turns to hobbies and I mention that mine is flying radio controlled gliders (or, as I prefer to call them, sailplanes), I can guarantee that three questions will be asked.

The first query is inevitably: 'But how can you have any control over them without an engine?' Totally illogical as this may seem, in view of the widespread knowledge and acceptance of full-size sailplanes, it is definitely a problem area for the layman. It usually takes quite a lot of explanation to convince people that the aerodynamic control of an aeroplane has absolutely nothing to do with that fan at the front (or the glorified vacuum-cleaner at the rear!), and that sailplanes are in fact powered—they are powered by gravity!

The next question is usually: 'How do you launch them?' The answer to this is in the plural—either we throw them off cliffs or tow them up like a kite. Again, not all that surprising for anyone who has any knowledge of full-size glider launching techniques, although the 'bungee', which is the equivalent to our throwing a model off a hill, is not much used in the full-size world these days. Usually the follow-up question is: 'Yes, but how do they *stay* up without an engine?' This one takes a lot longer to answer; it is not easy to quickly convey a grasp of the constant movement of the atmosphere and its multiplicity of causes. Often the revelation of 18 hour slope and 3½ hour thermal duration records is met with frank disbelief.

The conversation then usually relapses into: 'How do you land them' (my stock answer is: 'With great difficulty!') and: 'How far away can you control them?' (answer: 'How good is your eyesight?!') and so on.

It is my hope that this book will answer all these questions in full, and a lot more besides, and show anyone, no matter how slight their present knowledge, how to get started in the business of R/C glider flying. It is aimed, unashamedly, at the beginner, and my aim is that anyone reading it will find enough help to carry them past the critical and difficult stages of building and flying that first R/C sailplane, and provide them with inspiration for more advanced projects in the future.

Whilst there is nothing in the building of simple R/C soaring models which cannot be overcome with moderate manual dexterity, and a liberal application of commonsense, practical, on-the-spot, help is always useful. When it comes to the actual flying of the model, I would suggest that such assistance is near-vital if the beginner wishes to avoid damaging his carefully built model. For this reason, I would urge anyone to seek out the place where the local enthusiasts fly, join their club or association, ask for and, most of all, act upon advice.

Even a small radio control glider has the potential to cause damage to people or objects with which it may come into involuntary contact. With this in mind, proper vetting of the model before flights are attempted is essential, as is the presence of an experienced guiding hand to avoid disaster until the necessary skills are developed. It should also be remembered that the operator of any form of flying model aeroplane should be covered by adequate third-party insurance, and that flying should only take place on sites where the per-

mission of the landowner has been sought and obtained; joining a club is the simplest, and cheapest, way to ensure that the latter two conditions are met. Because they are silent, R/C gliders are the most environmentally acceptable form of radio controlled model aircraft, and they may be flown at sites which are far too noise sensitive to permit powered models. However, this must not be taken as licence to fly without permission or in unsuitable locations.

Because the intention of this book is to concentrate firmly on basic techniques, it will not be possible to include too much detail on advanced construction techniques, high performance models, advanced and contest flying etc. The amount of detail involved in the hobby can be appreciated by the fact that my book on just one aspect, 'Radio Controlled Thermal Soaring' (published by Chart Hobby Distributors Ltd) extends to almost 400 pages. This latter book, together with 'Radio Controlled Slope Soaring' from the same publishers and D. Jones' 'R/C Gliding' from Argus Books, can be recommended as further reading if more in-depth information is required.

However, no-one will learn how to fly, let alone how to soar effectively, solely from books. The secret is care and application in building, together with practical help in learning to fly. Enjoy your modelling!

Chapter 2
What are R/C gliders?

AS IMPLIED in the previous chapter, radio controlled sailplanes may be conveniently split into two main divisions, and then into several sub-divisions.

The principal division is between those models intended for *slope soaring* and those designed for *thermal soaring*. It will be seen later that this division is not absolutely clear-cut, for, whilst a

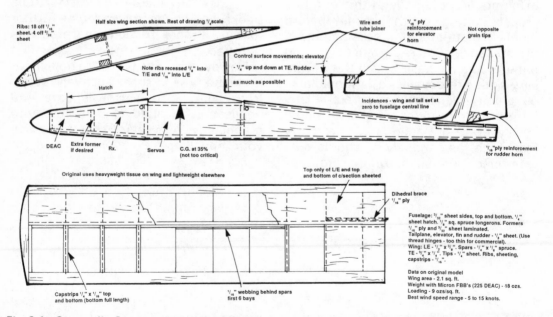

Ribs: 18 off $^1/_{16}$" sheet. 4 off $^3/_{32}$" sheet

Half size wing section shown. Rest of drawing $^1/_4$ scale

Note ribs recessed $^1/_4$" into T/E and $^1/_{16}$" into L/E

Wire and tube joiner

$^1/_{16}$" ply reinforcement for elevator horn

Not opposite grain tips

Control surface movements: elevator - $^1/_4$" up and down at TE. Rudder - as much as possible!

Incidences - wing and tail set at zero to fuselage central line

DEAC

Extra former if desired

Rx.

Servos

C.G. at 35% (not too critical)

$^1/_{16}$" ply reinforcement for rudder horn

Hatch

Original uses heavyweight tissue on wing and lightweight elsewhere

Top only of L/E and top and bottom of c/section sheeted

Dihedral brace $^1/_{16}$" ply

Fuselage: $^3/_{32}$" sheet sides, top and bottom. $^1/_4$" sheet hatch. $^1/_8$" sq. spruce longerons. Formers $^1/_{16}$" ply and $^3/_{32}$" sheet laminated.
Tailplane, elevator, fin and rudder - $^1/_4$" sheet. (Use thread hinges - too thin for commercial).
Wing: LE - $^1/_8$" x $^3/_8$". Spars - $^1/_8$" x $^1/_4$" spruce. TE - $^3/_4$" x $^1/_4$". Tips - $^1/_4$" sheet. Ribs, sheeting, capstrips - $^1/_{16}$".

Data on original model
Wing area - 2.1 sq. ft.
Weight with Micron FBB's (225 DEAC) - 18 ozs.
Loading - 9 ozs/sq. ft.
Best wind speed range - 5 to 15 knots.

Capstrips $^1/_8$" x $^1/_{16}$" top and bottom (bottom full length)

$^1/_{16}$" webbing behind spars first 6 bays

Fig. 2.1—Snoopy II—Compact slope trainer.

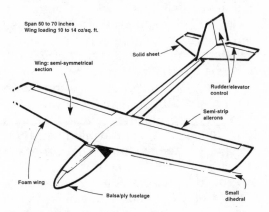

Span 50 to 70 inches
Wing loading 10 to 14 oz/sq. ft.

Wing: semi-symmetrical section

Solid sheet

Rudder/elevator control

Semi-strip ailerons

Foam wing

Balsa/ply fuselage

Small dihedral

Fig. 2.2 Aileron trainer.

specialist slope model is unlikely to be a very satisfactory thermal soaring performer when launched by tow-line, most thermal models are perfectly at home on the slope in the right conditions.

If the beginner attends a flying session at his local slope soaring site, he will see a bewildering variety of models being flown. These may be best broken down into a number of sub-categories, although once again it must be appreciated that the boundaries between some groups are rather blurred.

Fig. 2.1. One of the most common types seen will be the trainer, or sport model. This will typically be between 40 and 60 inches span, equipped with rudder and elevator control and will

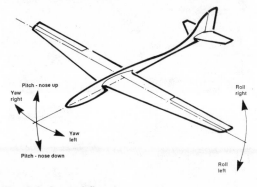

Pitch - nose up
Yaw right
Roll right
Yaw left
Pitch - nose down
Roll left

Fig. 2.3 Control fixes.

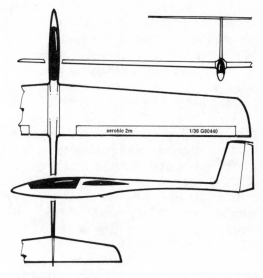

aerobic 2m   1/36 G80440

Fig. 2.4 Aerobic 2m.

normally be of fairly 'boxy' layout and rugged structure.

Fig. 2.2. A development of the trainer type, seen in the hands of the more experienced slope flyer, is the aileron trainer or intermediate aerobatic model. Normally of between 50 and 70 inches span, this will be of rather more refined aerodynamic layout than the basic trainer, and structurally may feature a fibreglass fuselage. The three main flight controls will be rudder, elevator and ailerons, and their functions are indicated in Fig. 2.3. Whilst models such as this will be capable of a reasonable range of aerobatics, and, with the use of ailerons, have better tight manoeuvring capability than a rudder/elevator model, they will not use a fully symmetrical wing section and will fall short of full aerobatic performance. Conversely, they will be capable of soaring in poorer lift conditions than the full aerobatic soarer.

Fig. 2.4. The aerobatic slope soarer, often referred to as the 'kipper'. These models are usually between 50 and 80 inches in span. They have large aileron control surfaces, plus rudder and elevator, and sometimes flaps linked to the elevator as an aid to tightening aerobatic manoeuvres. Aerobatic models are expected to fly as well inverted as they do upright, and to this end will usually feature a wing section with as much camber on the bottom as the top— the so-called 'symmetrical' section. Whilst improving the inverted flight performance and 'outside' manoeuvres, such a section does not generate as much lift as one having a greater camber on the top surface than the bottom, and hence the soaring performance of the kipper is not outstanding. In other words, to perform satisfactorily, they will require that the slope should be producing a reasonable amount of lift—see Chapter 5.

Fig. 2.5. The pylon racing model. Designed to fly as fast as possible, either in direct competition with one or more other models, or against the stop watch in the class of contest known as 'F3F', these models often appear superficially much like an aerobatic design, albeit rather larger. The resemblance is largely skin deep, however, since a pylon racer will use a slim, almost flat-bottomed wing section, and will often dispense with the rudder control function, relying on ailerons alone for directional control. In these circumstances turns are made by rolling the model onto its side with aileron and then 'pulling' it through the turn with up elevator. Racing models tend to be sleeker and slimmer than aerobatic designs, and also generally larger at 70 to 110 inches span. Very advanced constructional techniques involving glass, carbon and Kevlar fibres and specially moulded wings are sometimes used, and occasionally ailerons are replaced by a system which twists the whole of each wing for roll control.

Fig. 2.6. Cross-country soaring models. Designed to be flown around cross-country courses laid out on the hills, using both slope generated and thermal lift, these models are often very large, ranging from 120 to 180 inches span. They are normally very clean and sleek in layout, not unlike a full-size sailplane, and often feature full span flaps as well as aileron, elevator and rudder controls. They are relatively heavy, very efficient at using lift and covering ground be-

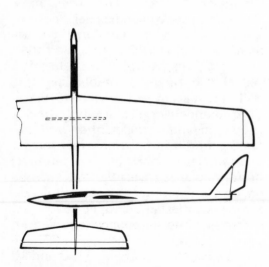

Fig. 2.5 Twist wing control pylon racer.

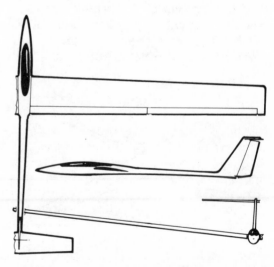

Fig. 2.6 Eclipse—Cross country model.

First, second and third in the first ever international cross-country contest show off models of 14 to 16 foot span.

tween turn points, and are often flown at the limit of vision and to great heights.

In addition to these types, and various unconventional models, such as tailless (all-wing) and delta wing designs, two types of scale model may also be observed. The first type, as expected, are scale replicas of full-size sailplanes, built to scales ranging from 1/6th to 1/3rd of the full size. Some of these are very large indeed, and all types of sailplane are modelled, from the very basic primary types of the 1920s and 1930s, through the wood-built high-performance types of the 1930s, 1940s and 1950s, to the very high performance 'glass ships' used in today's full-size gliding contests. Most of these models are beautifully built by expert modellers working from their own plans, but there are some practically ready-to-fly glass fibre scale models in 1/5th and 1/4 scale available—at a price! Preparing these for flight is virtually limited to fitting the radio gear—but, be warned, they are not for novice pilots, and a good deal of practice with smaller simpler models is required to prepare for this kind of flying.

Other scale models often seen on the slopes are more unexpected—they are glider models of powered full-size aircraft often, but not always, jets. Some of these 'P.S.S.' (power-slope-scale)

models are exact scale, but due to the small wing areas of present day jet aircraft many are 'caricatures' using larger than scale wings. However, when flown in good lift so that they can be moved around the sky quickly, they really look the part, and can be very exciting to fly.

As can be seen from the above, the range of models from which the experienced slope soaring pilot can choose is very large indeed, but everyone needs to walk before they can run, and if the novice asks around amongst the veterans present, he will find that they all began with a possibly unlovely, but tough and practical trainer model.

Upon examining the other major subdivision of R/C gliders, thermal soarers, the newcomer might discern less variety than in the slope types. This greater conformity of design and layout is a result of several factors. Firstly, in order to obtain a satisfying performance from the tow-line, a lower sinking speed is required than that which is acceptable for the average slope soaring model, which has the advantage of normally operating in air which is always rising. Secondly, design development in thermal soaring has been much more 'contest-led' than has been the case in slope soaring where the vast majority of flying done is 'sport flying' i.e. soaring for sheer enjoyment as opposed to flying for competitive purposes. This has naturally meant that published plan and kit designs for thermal soarers have all tended towards the shape and structures which are currently used on the contest circuit.

The vast majority of thermal soaring designs which are encountered will feature rudder as the principal directional control, with elevator, most often in the form of an 'all moving tailplane' rather than a separate hinged elevator. In addition, most models, certainly the larger ones, will have some form of airbrakes or spoilers. These are necessary to assist in accurately landing these models; without them the large amount of lift which the big flat-bottomed wings generate when the model is made to fly faster can cause considerable embarrassment to the pilot.

Duration type thermal soarers will also often feature wings with tip dihedral or polyhedral. Some form of dihedral, i.e the tips of the wings lifted in relation to the centre section, is absolutely necessary on all models which use rudder as the primary directional control, otherwise it will not be possible to turn the model properly, or even at all. However, rudder/elevator slope soarers most typically use 'straight' or 'V' dihedral, where the wing panel on each side is lifted in a straight line from the centre section. Although 'V' dihedral thermal soarers are seen, it has been found over the years that, for large span models, a dihedral pattern such as that shown in Fig. 2.7 will give superior handling characteristics.

Fig. 2.7 portrays the typical layout of a duration thermal soarer; this reasonably reflects the appearance of models from the four main classes of thermal model —mini-glider, two metre, standard class or 100S and open class. The principal difference between these classes is one of size.

A mini-glider has a maximum span of 60 inches and a maximum allowed weight of 20 ounces.

Two metre models have a maximum span of two metres (naturally!), but no other restrictions.

A 100S or standard class model, perhaps the most popular and often seen type of thermal soarer on the local club flying field, has a maximum span of 100 inches, may not use ailerons or flaps, but is otherwise unrestricted.

The open class model is not subject to any restrictions other than the maximum size and weight definitions applied to model aeroplanes under the FAI (Federation Aeronautique International) rules, that is 11 pounds maximum weight and 16 square feet area. Open models seen on British flying fields are typically from 130 to 180 inches span, and weigh between 4 and 8 pounds. Some of the larger ones do use aileron control, and occasionally flap controls as well. However, since the aim is not to perform aerobatics, these are only used to improve the precision of control of the large-span models, and the average open model is more usually a rudder/elevator controlled machine. It has been found that, in model sizes, aileron control movements on long-span models can cause great disruption to the airflow over the wing, and lead to loss of efficiency when flying slowly at the glider's minimum sinking speed. Since this is the flight regime in which the thermal soarer spends most of its time, ailerons are only favoured by a few designs.

The only thermal soarers which habitually use ailerons are those designed to compete in the multi-task, or 'F3B' contests, the international class of competition. Since these contests re-

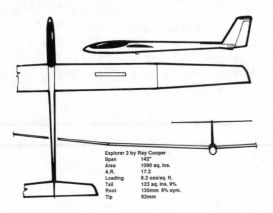

Fig. 2.7 Duration thermal soarer.

Explorer 2 by Ray Cooper	
Span	142"
Area	1090 sq. ins.
A.R.	17.2
Loading	8.2 ozs/sq. ft.
Tail	123 sq. ins. 9%
Root	135mm 8% sym.
Tip	82mm

quire that the model should perform not only duration but distance and speed tasks around a closed circuit, handling and manoeuvrability are important as well as sheer soaring performance. Hence a multi-task model will use ailerons, often combined full span aileron/flaps, sometimes with sophisticated radio functions to enable these to be used to vary the shape of the wing section in flight. As with slope aerobatic, pylon race and scale models, multi-task models are for the experienced modeller and pilot.

The best model for the thermal beginner is undoubtedly a plain two metre or 100S rudder/elevator design, possibly with airbrakes or spoilers. While the small size and cheapness of the mini-glider class (originally used for hand launch or 'chuck' glider competition) may at first appear attractive, they require careful building to keep the weight down and they also call for use of miniature radio equipment. In addition to these drawbacks, the smaller size makes it more difficult to extract really satisfying performances from these models, so although they are fun to fly and provide a challenge for the more experienced pilot, they are best left alone initially.

As was mentioned earlier, any reputable thermal soarer will also fly from the slope. This statement, however, requires a little qualification. The problems faced by a slope model—turbulence, rough and small landing areas, sometimes high winds—require certain quali-ties to combat them i.e good 'agile' handling, strength, reasonably small size and so on. The larger thermal models, whilst having the ability, especially if loaded with ballast, to penetrate high winds from the slope and soar effortlessly to great heights, will be inferior to the small slope model when it comes to tight manoeuvring and landing, and will be more likely to suffer damage. The multi-task, or F3B model, which is normally a fast, relatively heavily loaded, aileron equipped model, is an exception to the above, and a good model of this type makes an excellent and exciting slope-soarer; indeed many are used for slope pylon racing and speed contests. However, such models are well outside the capabilities of the novice builder and soaring pilot, so if the wind is blowing strongly enough to produce sufficient slope lift to enable a 'genuine' slope soarer to be flown, this will be the most satisfying option.

The thermal model, however, comes into its own in very light winds on the slope, when some fascinating flying can be had, making the best of what little slope lift there is available and using thermals which come through to climb away to great height.

It is clearly a case, then, of 'horses for courses'; the beginner who wishes to enjoy the best of both types of flying really needs two models, but if he had to make do with just one, then a sturdily built two metre thermal model would give him the most flying opportunities.

Chapter 3
Getting started

THIS CHAPTER will leave you with several suggested ways to start out on the task of becoming a proficient radio controlled soaring pilot. Since this book cannot claim to be an exhaustive work, they are not the only satisfactory routes which may be followed, and, once again, the importance of listening to and acting upon advice from an experienced modeller needs to be stressed.

Assuming that the reader is starting from scratch, with no previous modelling background, what will he or she need? The basic necessities are: a model which is suitable to the individual's purpose; a radio system of some sort to control it; various support equipment for the operation of the model and radio, some tools for use in the construction of the model, and a place to fly it.

Since there is nothing more frustrating than having a complete, ready-to-fly model and nowhere to fly it, the last item on this list is the place to start. As stated in Chapter 2, it is absolutely necessary that the complete newcomer find some local enthusiasts if he is to have a sporting chance of success, and this should help in providing the flying site, be it flat field or slope.

The next thing to consider is the radio. I would strongly advise that this is obtained first, since the size and layout of the airborne components is going to have some bearing on the building of the model. When looking in the model shop, or perusing the mail order advertisements in the model press, the number and variety of radio outfits available can be completely bewildering. All current radio sets are *proportional* types. This was not always the case, but delving into the past is no part of this particular book; just be grateful that we live in an enlightened electronic age. Basically, in a proportional radio, one *servo* is physically connected (via a push-rod, wire linkage or bowden cable) to each control surface. This servo is in turn electronically connected to one output channel of the receiver. The receiver is powered by an airborne battery pack, normally of 4.8 or 6 volts, which also supplies the power to drive the servos. All this equipment is contained in the model and comprises the *airborne system*.

The transmitter has a number of function controls which correspond to the output channels of the receiver, the controls themselves consisting of spring centred levers or 'sticks' for the main flying controls and positionable levers or toggle switches for subsidiary functions. Radios are available with varying numbers of control channels—the normal ones found being 2, 4, 6 and 8 channel. A two channel radio will normally be equipped with two single axis sticks, the right-hand one moving from left to right, the left hand one at 90 degrees to this, from top to bottom. A two channel set will thus provide rudder and elevator controls for a simple glider.

On sets with four or more channels, the normal control layout is two dual axis sticks, one of which is spring centred on both axes, while the other has a spring centred left to right axis and a positionable (ratchet) vertical axis. Each of the main controls is provided with a subsidiary, non self-centring, 'trim' lever, by means of which the neutral, or central position of each control may be varied.

Since this is 'proportional' radio, the movement of the servo in the model, and hence the control surface to which it is linked, follows precisely the movement of the appropriate control stick on the transmitter—it is as simple as that. What is rather less simple to understand is that there are two completely different transmitter layouts for the principal controls used by glider pilots in this country. The reasons for this are rooted back in modelling antiquity; suffice to say that 'Mode 1' indicates that the principal directional control (rudder in the case of a rudder/elevator model, ailerons in the case of an aileron model) and the pitch control—elevator —are operated by separate sticks. Since all two channel outfits currently on the market have separate sticks for the two control functions, they are naturally of the Mode 1 type. With four channel sets, the transmitters are available with the ratchet function on either the right-hand (Mode 1) or left-hand (Mode 2) stick. From this you will deduce that Mode 2 pilots fly with the principal flying controls on one stick (the right-hand one in the case of right-handed people).

You will hear violent arguments about which is the 'right' mode. Mode 1 protagonists will argue that, with the principal controls on separate sticks there is no chance of inadvertent interaction between them. Mode 2 pilots will counter with the statement that 'their' method is more akin to full-size practice. By now the beginner will be totally confused; which mode should *he* use?

There is no hard and fast answer; in my view it is entirely down to individual circumstances. The three most important deciding factors are:

Is your radio equipment a two channel set with two separate control sticks, as for instance, all the outfits used for electric R/C cars? If the answer is 'yes', then you have no choice but to fly two stick or Mode 1.

Are you one of those people who is completely 'one-handed' (like myself); in other words your left hand (or right hand, if you are left-handed) is only really useful for holding things? If so then you will probably adapt more readily to one stick, or Mode 2.

What system do the majority of experienced soarers use in the group you have joined? This will vary with geographical locality, there being Mode 1 and Mode 2 'strongholds' up and down the country. From the beginners' point of view, there are obviously great advantages to flying the mode which is most popular with his potential instructors.

Assuming you have sorted out the above there is one more consideration; which frequency band? In the UK there are three frequency bands in use for R/C modelling; 35 MHz for model flying only; 40 MHz for surface vehicles; and 27 MHz shared between both flying and surface models. Most of the very inexpensive two channel sets around are aimed at R/C cars, so although such a set is entirely adequate for a two function (rudder/elevator) glider, the odds are it will be on the 27 MHz frequency. Whilst this may be acceptable for flying from the slope, where the site is usually remote from the populated areas in which most model car operation takes place, it could hardly be recommended for flying from most thermal soaring fields. Should someone nearby switch on an R/C car on the same 'spot' frequency as your equipment, your model would crash.

On the whole, the use of 35 MHz equipment is strongly recommended for aircraft modelling, and such use is assumed throughout the rest of this book. Also, while a two channel set may appear, at first, to offer an attractive saving in cost over a four or six channel outfit, this will prove to be false economy if advancement to models using ailerons and/or airbrakes is envisaged. On the whole, my recommendation would be to buy a 35 MHz, four or six channel transmitter and receiver, with just two servos to start with. This will not be greatly more expensive than a two channel set, and additional servos can be purchased as required.

It should be explained at this point that the allocated frequency band is divided into a number of 'spot' frequencies, spaced 10 KHz apart. Each of these spots is identified by a number, ranging from 60 to 84, and this must be displayed on a pennant flown on the transmitter aerial. Only one transmitter on a particular spot frequency may be operated at once. *Never switch your transmitter on until you are sure that no-one else is flying on 'your' spot frequency*. Most club flying fields have frequency control, centred on the use of a clothes peg carrying the channel (spot) number, which must be in the possession of the modeller before he switches on his radio. However, some slope sites, even when there are quite large numbers of flyers present, do not use any form of control, and there are variations in the basic method in use, so *always ask before switching on*.

One other question which needs to be resolved with regard to the radio is that of batteries. Most of the less expensive sets are, these days, supplied for dry battery operation, with an option to fit rechargeable nickel-cadmium batteries as an extra. Whilst dry-battery operation is a practical proposition, it can become expensive over a period of time, and better economy and safety of operation is provided by using rechargeables. To simplify matters, it is best to buy the rechargeable conversion set specially produced for your particular radio—this may work out a little more expensive than buying separate batteries and charger, but it safeguards the warranty on the equipment, and ensures that the charger is providing the correct current.

Finally, on radio selection; there are some very sophisticated—and expensive—'computer' radios now available. While these provide superb facilities for the advanced modeller wishing to mix several functions, program-in settings for different models and so on, they are neither necessary, nor even desirable, for the beginner in R/C soaring.

The next major consideration is a model...and this is where things start to become really complicated! If the soaring newcomer is a complete novice in the art of building flying model aeroplanes, then it may be worth considering the possibility of acquiring a ready-built model, either second-hand from an experienced enthusiast, or as an 'almost ready to fly' type from a model shop. I am hesitant in advising this course to all except the most ham-fisted of novices, for a number of reasons.

On a personal note, the creation of the model is surely one of the most satisfying parts of this hobby; it has to be said that there is a tendency to treat something which has been created with one's own hands with a great deal more care than something which has simply cost money. However, this may be viewed as prejudice, and far more important is the fact that, if the newcomer is to progress to any great extent in the hobby, and extract maximum enjoyment from it, sooner or later he will have to build his own models—so it is perhaps best to start from the word go!

If we assume, then, that the beginner is to build his own first model, we find that a number of routes are open to him. Once again, however, the way in which any individual will progress depends to a great extent upon his experience and manual dexterity. For the newcomer who has absolutely no experience of aeromodelling, there is no doubt that the best starting point is a kit model. Building from a kit he will find (usually) reasonably comprehensive instructions provided and, in addition, many of the accessories and small items which he will need to complete the model will be in the kit. A further additional, and considerable, advantage is that, in any reputable kit, the important parts will be cut or machined accurately to shape, assisting the less experienced in producing a well aligned structure.

There are drawbacks, however, to building from a kit. The first is that, in some instances, features which may be desirable will have been omitted from the design, or modified, to either hold down cost or make the process of kitting easier. Secondly, the selection of materials, in particular balsa wood, by a kit manufacturer, does not, in some cases, match that which an individual modeller can achieve; admittedly, this is not so relevant in the case of the beginner who will not have the necessary skills to choose his own wood in any event. Thirdly, a model produced from a kit will inevitably be more expensive than the same model produced from a plan and materials. On the whole, however, the raw beginner would do well to choose a kit. A selection of glider kits currently available in the UK is shown in Table 1. This is not exhaustive, and as new models are added (older kits go out of production all the time), it may be of only limited assistance.

Table 1 Glider Kits

(This is not meant to be a comprehensive list; neither is inclusion in the list intended to imply that I recommend a particular kit. It is merely an indication of some names to look out for in the press and model shops. All the kits listed here were advertised as being available in mid 1989).

Beginners Slope
Middle Phase II
Aileron Middle Phase

Table 1 continued

Osprey 64
Impala
Super Snipe
Ridge Recruit
Rookie 68
Cub
Eagle
Simpleton
Apex 74

Beginners Thermal
Algebra 2.5M
Osprey 64
Osprey 100
Gentle Lady
Sunrise
Rookie 86
Sophisticated Lady
Vortex
Silver Cloud
Gold Cloud
Simple Sailman
Apex 98

Advanced Slope
Phase 6
Secret Weapon
Blob
Heron
Ridge Racer
Axle
Mini Racer
Sitar Special
Algebra 2.5M Aileron

Advanced Thermal
Topaz
Algebra 2.5M
Algebra 3M
Algebra 4M
Algebra 1000
Preacherman
Diamond Cloud
MultiPhase (semi kit)

There is no substitute for practical advice from one or more experienced soarers on the kit which is being considered. It is also a fact that almost all models have some weaknesses, and a little advice about such points during building is worth its weight in gold.

Twenty years ago, the advice to 'ask at your local model shop' would have been very sound, since most shops were run, or at least staffed, by enthusiasts who could give sound and helpful guidance. However, the inevitable rise of the discount mail-order dealers, changes in economic circumstances, and the trend towards R/C model cars as the 'mass' model 'toy' means that there are now fewer of the kind of model shop which can really help the beginner, rather than just 'move boxes'. If you are lucky enough to have one of the old-fashioned type in your area—make use of the proprietor's knowledge, and in return help him to stay in business by buying your modelling requirements from him, even if it means paying a few pounds more for your radio than you might from the discount dealer.

If, as is the case with many people new to R/C soaring, the soaring beginner has some experience of building model aircraft in the past, then the choice open to him will be wider, since such a person will probably have the necessary background to tackle the building of his first model from a plan, buying the necessary materials as required in the form of sheet and strip balsa, spruce and ply. Argus Specialist Publications offer a wide range of plans for R/C gliders, and additional ones are published at frequent intervals in their magazines *Radio Control Models and Electronics (R.C.M. & E.)* and *Radio Modeller (R.M.)*.

Nowadays, since many models use wings made from polystyrene foam covered in hardwood veneer, there is a further choice available. This takes the form of the 'wings and plan pack', where a pair of foam/veneered wings, ready for joining and finishing, are supplied together with a plan of fuselage and tail surfaces, leaving the builder to obtain the materials to build these himself. Sometimes, a glass fibre fuselage is available as well, but in my view, glass fibre models are best avoided as first soarers, due to the difficulty of repairing such fuselages! This may strike the reader as a pessimistic viewpoint, but rest assured it is born out of experience!

Looking now at the *type* of model which the *ab initio* soarer will need; as outlined in Chapter 2, this depends upon whether his initial flying outings are to be from the slope or on the flat field. Unless, for reasons of geography, a slope is not conveniently available, I would recommend that slope flying is the quickest way to get a reasonable number of hours of air time within a short period. There are drawbacks to this approach; it is always much more difficult to land a model safely on a slope than on a flat field, but generally slope models can be made tougher to offset this. Once the necessary basic control skills have been learned, the new pilot can then venture onto the flat field with every confidence, since the actual *flying* will be easier than on the slope, due to the generally less turbulent conditions and easier landings. This will enable him to concentrate on acquiring the new skills of handling a model during a tow-launch and, most difficult of all, finding and using thermal lift.

My personal recommendation, then, for a first model, would be a tough, reasonably compact (40 to 50 inch) rudder/elevator slope trainer type. This should be of either all-wood construction, or foam/veneered wings with a wooden fuselage and tail surfaces. Full details of recommended constructional and finishing methods for such a model will be found in a later chapter.

As a follow-up model to this, a simple, all-wood, two metre or preferably 100S thermal model could be started as soon as the first one is completed. By the time the novice has learned to fly on his slope model, the second model should then be ready. This will serve the dual purpose of enabling him to fly in lighter conditions on the slope, when the lift is not strong enough to sustain his fairly inefficient trainer, and also initiating him into flat field flying. It will come as a surprise to the modeller to find that a glider of this type is considerably easier to fly than his slope trainer, leading to the thought that perhaps the building order of these two models could have been reversed. However, this is not so, since, while actually more docile and easier to control, the bigger model will certainly not 'bounce' out of crashes like the smaller, tougher slope soarer, and the real reason that the modeller finds the former easy to fly is that he has mastered the latter!

It is difficult to be too specific on the question of the tools and support equipment which will be required for the creation and maintenance of the models. Many people will already be well equipped with do-it-yourself tools, and most of these will find some application in modelling. The only really specialist tools required are:

A good modelling knife; the specially produced type is adequate, and comes into its own for cutting ply and spruce, but for balsa there is no better knife than a medical scalpel with several packets of variously shaped blades.

One or more razor saws.

Junior hacksaw.

Sanding block and several grades of sandpaper.

Pins, tape, bulldog clips and spring clothes pegs.

Of course, as the modeller progresses he will discover other needs; for example, although it is possible to use the domestic electric iron when covering with heat-shrink film or fabric, a much better (and easier) job results from the use of a lightweight tacking iron and heat-gun. However, the need for these additional items will become self-evident to the modeller as he progresses through the various stages of the hobby.

If your radio equipment is equipped with rechargeable batteries, then the appropriate charger will be required. Most manufacturers of radio equipment supply chargers for their gear featuring dual outputs, one each for the transmitter (which is normally 9.6 volts) and the receiver (4.8 volts). These chargers are set up to give a safe 'trickle' charge rate which is usually 10% of the rated capacity of the cells; for example, the trickle charge for 500 MAh (half ampere hour) cells is 50 milliamps. Although it is perfectly possible to use other chargers, provided they are equipped with a control to vary the charge and an ammeter to facilitate setting it, for safety's sake, it is best to stick with the manufacturer's charger.

Whilst many cells in use today are of the 'vented' type and will therefore accept rapid charges at high currents, great care is required since overcharging at high rates will ruin cells, and indeed may cause them to explode violently with dire consequences to the surroundings. In general, I would recommend sticking to trickle charging, when a full charge will take 10 to 14 hours, and, at these rates, no damage will result if the cells are accidentally left connected for twice this period.

Do remember that batteries lose capacity whilst sitting around doing nothing. If you charge the equipment one weekend and then do not fly it until the following weekend, do give it a further charge, of, say, 5 or 6 hours duration before going out.

Present day radio equipment gives remarkably little trouble, and the majority of problems encountered are traced to the batteries; care for these vital components and treat them with respect, and you will reap the benefit of long, trouble-free service from your equipment.

Chapter 4
Building a first slope or thermal soarer

THIS CHAPTER will concentrate on the structural methods and techniques which are likely to be encountered by the modeller in building a straightforward all wood, or foam wing/wooden fuselage model from a kit or plan.

The first thing to remember is the old adage 'if all else fails, read the instructions'. This may not be universally applicable, since, if working from a plan, the modeller may well not have the past issue of the magazine wherein the design, and the accompanying building instructions, were published. In this case it is worth asking around clubmates in the hope that one of them will be able to loan the appropriate issue. Failing this, asking an experienced modeller to run over the plans, suggest an assembly sequence and point out any possible pitfalls, is something which can often save a great deal of time and trouble. If building from a kit, one naturally expects to find instructions included, but it has to be said that these

do vary from really excellent to sketchy in the extreme.

First of all, a few general comments about desirable features of that first model.

Whether the aim is slope or thermal flying, a design which has at least the wing, and possibly also the tail, held in place by good old-fashioned rubber bands, in the manner used by free-flight modellers since time immemorial, has much to commend it. When compared with the bolt-on wings of more advanced slope soarers, and the plug-in multi-part wings used by most thermal models, this may seem decidedly crude; however, the advantages of such a flexible arrangement will be clearly demonstrated on the first occasion when, travelling at high speed, the model meets an immovable object, such as the ground!

Following similar reasoning, although two-part wings, usually joined by wire rods, are a useful transport aid, it would be best if a first model, at least up to two metres in size, were to use a one-piece wing. This eliminates a prime area for mis-alignment and considerably simplifies the wing construction. If the first model is a 100S type, which, for practical reasons, really does need a two-part wing, then the type which joins together with one or more wire dowels on the centre-line and is then strapped onto the fuselage with rubber bands as a one-piece unit is to be preferred. Wings which plug in on either side of the fuselage require much more careful and accurate workmanship if difficulties such as having each wing half at a slightly different angle of incidence are to be avoided, and are also more susceptible to crash damage.

Fuselages should be uncompromisingly slab-sided—streamlined structures are harder to build, make radio installation more difficult and are often not as

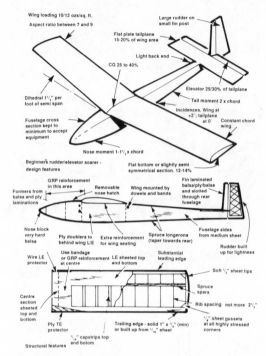

Fig. 4.1 Desirable design and construction features of beginner's rudder/slope soarer.

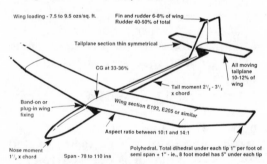

Fig. 4.2 Desirable design and construction features of beginner's thermal soarer.

Straightforward two metre models are useful for both slope and thermal soaring. This is Sean Bannister with his 'Algebra 2M' prototype.

strong. While tapered wings and tail surfaces are good practice on more advanced models, giving advantages in weight distribution and drag reduction, constant chord wings make for easier and hence more accurate construction and are entirely satisfactory for models whose main purpose is training, particularly in the case of the short-span slope soaring model.

Figs. 4.1 and 4.2 show, after taking all

the above and many other points into account, what I consider to be the ideal layout for a first slope and first thermal model. Naturally, available kits and plans will not all conform exactly to this layout—different designers often follow different routes to the same destination. However, in most of the designs recommended as being suitable for beginners, you will find many of the features of these 'theoretical' models. Remember, at this stage of the game you are not interested in contest performance—the requirements are strength, stability, repairability and an adequately good flying performance.

Building your model

It will be necessary to generalise in this section; obviously the particular plan or kit selected will have detailed constructional points which cannot be covered here—which is why it is necessary to carefully read the instructions. However, the following sections will cover most of the general constructional techniques which will be encountered in models which are suitable for the novice.

Wings

The heart of any aeroplane is the wing—the item which provides the lift and makes flight possible at all. If the wing is misshapen or warped the model will not fly well—it may not even fly at all. If the wing structure is poorly designed or carelessly executed, resulting in inadequate strength, the model may fly—but not for long!

In order to provide lift the wing must have an aerofoil section—the ones found on trainer type models will generally be flat on the underside (or in some cases slightly concave i.e. 'undercambered') and convex on the upper surface. It is this shape which enables the surface to generate useful quantities of lift as it moves through the air. Wing sections are a subject with which the soaring pilot will become very familiar in his later progress through more advanced models; however, for the types under consideration, a basically flat bottomed section with a maximum thickness of around 10 to 12 percent of the wing chord, and with the leading edge rounded out underneath to give a 'raised nose entry' to the section, will be ideal—and easy to build!

There are three types of structure which the embryo glider pilot is likely to encounter—foam/veneer, foam/spar (not veneered) and built-up rib and spar, with partial or total balsa sheet covering. All are satisfactory and straightforward; perhaps the foam types make it easier for the beginner to produce an accurate wing.

Foam/veneer wings usually come in two separate panels, with the veneer skin ready bonded to the pre-cut foam cores. Building (or, perhaps more correctly in this case, assembling) the wings requires that balsa leading and trailing (front and rear) spars be bonded to the panels, and the panels then joined together at the appropriate dihedral angle. The fitting of block or sheet balsa tips and final sanding to shape then results in a wing ready for covering.

It is necessary, when working with foam wing panels, to exercise care about the type of adhesives used; epoxies and PVA glues are fine, but balsa cement, polyester resins, cyanoacrylate 'super glue' and any form of cellulose must be avoided, since all these attack and dissolve polystyrene foam. (This also means that, if the wing is to be finished with cellulose dope, the surface must be sealed with no cracks or crevices which will allow the dope to penetrate below the veneer skin.)

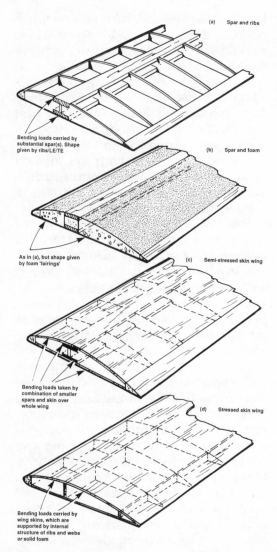

Bending loads carried by substantial spar(s). Shape given by ribs/LE/TE

(b)   Spar and foam

As in (a), but shape given by foam 'fairings'

(c)   Semi-stressed skin wing

Bending loads taken by combination of smaller spars and skin over whole wing

(d)   Stressed skin wing

Bending loads carried by wing skins, which are supported by internal structure of ribs and webs *or* solid foam

Fig. 4.3 (a) Spar and ribs. (b) Spar and foam. (c) Semi-stressed skin wing. (d) Stressed skin wing.

While a simple butt centre joint, reinforced with a wrapping of fibreglass bandage and resin, is fine for the one piece 40 to 60 inch wing of a typical slope trainer, the bigger foam/veneer wings for use on a thermal model require rather different treatment. The whole of the strength of a foam/veneer wing is in its skin—it is a 'stressed skin' structure. If the wing is to be made in two pieces, therefore, some method of transferring the loads from the metal joiners to the skin *must* be employed, or the wing will surely fail. The simplest way to achieve this is to mount the joiner tubes on ply 'webs' which are slotted into each wing half, the ply being considerably longer than the joiner.

If, despite its size, the thermal model wing is still to be a one piece structure, the glued and bandaged centre joint may be used, but to withstand the extra stresses imposed by tow-line operation, the wing should also be slotted to accept one or more full depth ply dihedral braces which are solidly glued in place during the joining process. Naturally, these braces must be cut to include the required dihedral angle, and rather than one thick (1/8th inch) brace, it is much better to use two thinner (1/16th inch) ones of differing lengths, the longer one at the thickest part of the wing chord and the other some two or three inches nearer the trailing edge, to provide a graduated reduction in strength with distance from the centre.

The foam/spar wing differs from the foam/veneer type in a number of important ways. Firstly it incorporates a 'proper' wing spar to take most of the bending loads imposed on the structure. Because of this, if the foam cores are made from a denser than normal foam, known as 'blue' foam or, more properly, styrofoam, the surface veneer can be replaced by a lighter skinning of tissue, heat-shrink plastic, or, perhaps most satisfactory of all, ordinary gift-wrapping paper applied with wallpaper paste and finished with polyurethane varnish!

Construction of a foam/spar wing is simplicity itself. The spar is built first; it is a full-depth structure, usually a composite of spruce top and bottom booms with balsa, or even foam, centre webs. For a two-part wing, the main wing-joiner tubes are built into the root end of each spar, which is appropriately reinforced with ply webs. In the case of a one piece wing, the spars are simply joined by ply dihedral braces (as are the outer dihedral breaks of a polyhedral wing). The pre-cut foam front and rear fairings, one of each for each panel, are then glued to the front and rear of the spar, and balsa leading and trailing edges glued to the front of these. Carving and sanding the balsa edges to the finished section, plus a general overall sanding, then completes the wing ready for covering.

In general, it is anticipated that, if he decides to use foam wings, the beginner will purchase the wing panels for his first few models either as part of a kit, or from one of the specialist services which offers to cut and skin wing panels for plan models. However, many more experienced modellers do cut their own wing panels; the equipment to do this (an electric foam cutting 'bow' and transformer) can be purchased for little cost, and there is nothing particularly difficult about the cutting of cores and skinning them to form finished panels.

The alternative to the foam wing is a wing built in the traditional aeromodelling style from balsa ribs, leading and trailing edge members and either balsa or spruce spars. This may be partially or entirely skinned in sheet balsa. This option may at first seem to involve much more work than a foam wing; this impression is rather misleading, however, and in real terms the difference in building time between the two types is not great. The built-up wing is, perhaps, less tolerant of inaccurate construction than the foam variety, but this is offset somewhat by the fact that a badly assembled, warped, foam wing is virtually impossible to correct, while its built-up equivalent can usually be salvaged. On the other hand, a built-up wing will usually have better weight and

strength distribution (stronger near the centre where strength is required, lighter near the tips) and be easier to repair.

In common with all basic aeromodelling structures the built-up wing is built over the plan to ensure accuracy. This introduces one of the most important 'tools' for the modeller— a good building board. Although essential for built-up wings, a true board of adequate size is also a great help when assembling a foam wing to ensure absolute accuracy.

There are a number of ways to obtain a suitable building board; perhaps most suitable of all, but most difficult to obtain, is a piece of slate bed from a snooker or pool table, with a sheet of 'K' quality hardboard (not to be confused with ordinary hardboard, the 'K' quality is a dense but relatively soft material about ½ inch thick which accepts and holds a pin pushed into it) or Sundeala board firmly bonded to it. A piece of thick plate glass with bevelled edges is equally suitable as a base, but failing these, a section of thick, postformed, veneered kitchen worktop can be used. These boards will have one thing in common—they will be *heavy*! A lighter, although possibly less satisfactory option, is a section of a cheap hardboard skinned, honeycomb centre internal door, once again faced with a suitable soft building surface.

The completed board should sit on a level bench surface; if your bench is not level insert packing pieces until the board rests solidly in place. Do take the trouble to obtain an adequate building surface—warped or twisted boards produce warped or twisted models, with the inevitable results. I use a 60 inch by 20 inch piece of 'K' hardboard glued and then screwed at 6 inch intervals around the edge to a 72 inch by 20 inch base of 1¼ inch thick high density laminate covered chipboard, the exposed foot of chipboard forming a convenient cutting surface. The finished board almost requires the services of a crane to move it, but it is certainly flat!

To return to the actual wing; construction will be commenced by pinning down the plan on the building board, and covering it with a sheet of polythene. The wing to be constructed will normally be of either the 'V' dihedral (2 panels), tip dihedral (3 panels) or polyhedral (4 panels) type. Whichever type is to be built, the panels will be constructed one at a time, flat over the appropriate section of the plan. If panels are to be permanently joined (as in the centre of a one piece 'V' dihedral wing, or at the tip dihedral breaks of a polyhedral one), then it is best to build the second panel onto the first, with the completed panel propped up to the correct dihedral angle.

The conventional wing structure will consist of a number of longitudinal members: leading edge (LE), trailing edge (TE), spar or spars, plus, in many cases, some full length surface sheeting, and the chordwise members at 90 degrees to these which form the shape of the wing section, the ribs. There will also be an ancillary structure such as webbing between vertically disposed

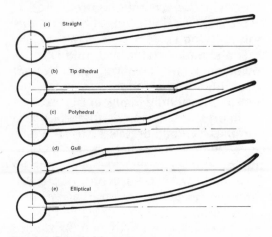

Fig. 4.4 Dihedral layouts.

pairs of spars, and possibly also between 'hollow' sheet top and bottom trailing edges, additional structure to take the joining tubes for two-part wings, and additional surface sheeting at the centre of the wings. Needless to say, fit of the parts together is of primary importance in producing a strong wing. If a part does not fit properly, resist the temptation to fill the gap with adhesive and instead cut a replacement part which *does* fit, the end result will be considerably stronger—and lighter.

Very often, in the areas of the wing which are not sheeted, the ribs have thin strips of sheet—capstrips—fitted to the top and bottom, effectively forming a 'T' section. These capstrips not only strengthen the rib considerably, but also provide more surface to which the covering material may adhere.

The normal sequence of assembly for a built-up wing is to pin out all the bottom surface sheeting and the bottom capstrips over the plan, together with the leading edge and trailing edge. Naturally, if the bottom surface of the wing is not perfectly flat, some members will have to be packed up from the plan to place them in the correct vertical location. Usually the leading edge will need to be raised from the plan, or as an alternative, an over-depth piece of balsa may be used and later carved back to size. If a section with a concave or undercambered underside is used, the trailing edge and bottom capstrips will require packing up to conform with the bottom rib contours. This can be rather tricky to get exactly right, and for this reason if no other a substantially flat-bottomed wing section is ideal for a first model.

The bottom spar (or spars in the case of a multi-spar wing) is the next item; this is glued and pinned down on top of the capstrips and bottom sheeting. All the ribs are then added, followed by details such as tubes at the root to take joiner rods in the case of a two-part wing, or dihedral braces for a single-part wing. The spar webbing is also added at this stage; this is one of the most tedious parts of built-up wing construction, but the webbing is very important since it adds enormous strength and rigidity to the wing. For this reason, it must be cut and fitted carefully, and this task will be much easier if the webbing pieces are cut from a constant width strip of balsa, and the webs and ribs added one at a time, working outward along the wing.

When the adhesive on all the above structure is dry, the top spar may be added, checking carefully that the spar webbing does not protrude above the level of the ribs, preventing the spar from fitting properly into the rib notches, and correcting where necessary. All the top surface sheeting and capstrips come next, pinning, gluing and taping these in place to conform with the curve of the top of the ribs. If the sheet is reluctant to bend over the ribs and stay in place, it will help to dampen the outside only of each piece with water. Similarly, cap-strips may be pre-curved by drawing them carefully under a pencil held down lightly on the bench a couple of times.

Once one complete wing panel is dry, if a second panel is to be joined onto it, the completed panel can be removed from the plan and jigged into the correct location to enable the second panel to be built directly onto it at the correct dihedral angle.

Further details such as an additional leading edge strip for carving to section, ply facing ribs at the roots in the case of two piece wings and fibreglass root reinforcement may now be added before giving the finished wing a thorough sanding to remove any bumps and reduce it to an accurate representation of the intended aerofoil section.

Fuselages

Turning to fuselages, the option is usually between a built-up unit, and a moulded fibreglass shell. Although the fibreglass approach may at first seem attractive, I would strongly recommend that a first model should use a wooden fuselage. There are problems in the fitting out of a fibreglass fuselage which may not at first be apparent to the beginner, and, in absolute terms, the strength/weight ratio of a wooden structure can be much better, and it will also be much easier to repair.

The normal structure which will be encountered, and the one which pro-duces the most satisfactory results for a first model, will be of sheet balsa sides, top and bottom, reinforced at the front with 'doublers' of thin plywood glued to the inside surfaces, and with longerons (usually spruce) running the full length in each corner. A number of rectangular formers, of balsa or balsa and ply laminated construction are used to join the sides.

When building this type of fuselage, the first step is to prepare a pair of sides by cutting out the basic shape in sheet balsa and laminating the doublers to the inside (beware at this stage—it is very easy to make two identical, e.g. left, sides—I have done this on more than one occasion!). The best adhesive for this is a contact type, preferably one of those which allows a certain amount of 'shuffling' to be done before the ad-hesive 'grips'. The longerons should also be glued in place at this stage, and the position of the formers marked carefully on the inside of each fuselage side.

Assembly of the fuselage, using the sides and formers, is best carried out using some kind of jig to ensure that the finished product is straight. Failing this, a centre line should be drawn on the building board, and centre marks placed on each of the formers to enable careful line-up during assembly. Addition of top and bottom sheeting and a block nose piece completes the basic fuselage (note that it is sometimes wise to install the drive linkages for the rudder and elevator, and perhaps even install the servos themselves before completely sheeting the top and bottom of the fuselage).

Usually, a hatch will be required in the top of the nose area to permit access to the radio equipment; the easiest way to fit this is to incorporate it as part of the fuselage main structure, and then cut it away after the fuselage has been carved and sanded to finished shape. Retention of the hatch can be via an internal rubber band, clip or magnetic catches, or even by plastic adhesive tape.

Tail surfaces

Very often the tail surfaces of the type of model under consideration will be simple flat balsa sheet structures. If this is the case, it is worthwhile including 'keys' or inserts whose grain runs at right-angles to that of the main pieces of sheet to help prevent warping. Alternatively, the surfaces may be constructed from strip balsa, in which case they are simply assembled over the plan in the same way as the wing.

There are many commercial plastic hinges available for attaching the movable rudder and elevator control surfaces to the tailplane and fin. Perhaps the best and simplest of these for the beginner is a series of small strips of thin Mylar sheet. The edges of the fixed and moving surfaces are carved and sanded to a 'V' along their centre lines and then slotted to take the Mylar strips. These are fitted in place and then 'pinned' by drilling clean through the surface and hinge and gluing a length of cocktail

stick in place, which is subsequently cut and sanded flush with the surface. These 'pins' are essential, since Mylar is very difficult to stick, and if the hinges are simply held into the slots with glue, they may well come adrift in flight with disastrous consequences.

This concludes a brief summary of how to build a basic wood or wood and foam airframe. The same techniques apply whether the model is a slope or thermal soarer. However, there are certain special considerations for each type which are summarised in the following paragraphs.

For a typical rudder/elevator slope soarer, *strength* is going to be of paramount importance, since much of its flying time will be spent in relatively high winds and, due to the rough nature of the terrain on many slopes, a good deal of involuntary contact with the ground and such unforgiving objects as rocks and dry stone walls is likely to occur in the early stages of its career. Consequently, some reinforcing of the front area of the fuselage is worthwhile, and this is most easily achieved by covering the inside with a layer of

Winter slope soaring demands lots of protective clothing, but can be very invigorating. Model is a rudder/elevator aerobatic glider.

fibreglass mat and resin. It is also worthwhile to use a spruce capping on the leading edge of such a model to resist nicks and chips, and a substantial spruce skid under the nose can sometimes absorb quite a lot of impact.

When considering a thermal soarer, the stresses involved are rather different. Although it is likely that landings will take place on a fairly smooth surface, there is considerable strain placed on the wings at the other end of the flight—the launch. Two of the areas of prime concern in the structure of the thermal model, therefore, must be firm and solid installation of the tow hook and adequate strength of the wing centre section. If the model has a one piece wing, as might be the case with a two metre or smaller model, then the centre section must have adequate ply bracing built in to give the necessary strength—and equally important, this bracing must not end suddenly, but must taper out towards the mid point of each wing panel.

With the more common two-part wings used on thermal soarers of above two metres span, the wire joining dowels will impart some degree of 'give' or 'spring' which will help to absorb the towing loads. However, it is even more essential in this case that the structure carrying the tubes which accommodate the joining dowels should taper out from the end of the wires, thus avoiding a sudden change in the strength of the wing.

With regard to the tow hook; it is not advisable to simply bolt this to the fuselage bottom, otherwise you may well find the bottom of the fuselage and the rest of the aeroplane going in different directions during a hefty tow-launch! A really substantial ply base, or hardwood block, preferably locked into a main former and/or the fuselage sides is required.

Covering and finishing

The options available these days for the covering and finishing of a glider are almost bewildering. The principal materials and techniques are:

Solid surfaces (i.e. veneered or fully sheeted wings)

Tissue and dope
Nylon and dope
Heat-shrink film covering
Heat-shrink fabric covering (with or without dope)
Glasscloth and epoxy resin covering

Open frame surfaces

Nylon and dope
Heat-shrink film covering
Heat-shrink fabric covering (with or without dope)

For the purposes of this book, where beginners' models are being considered, the use of epoxy resin and glasscloth is being ignored. This is an excellent technique, and with practice can produce outstanding results, but it is best left until the modeller has acquired a little experience.

For a slope soarer which will be subjected to a good deal of knocks and scuffs, the best choice is probably either nylon and dope or heat-shrink fabric, while for a thermal soarer, a solid surfaced wing could do far worse than to use tissue and dope, with heat-shrink film as a good option, and heat-shrink fabric coming into its own for the 100 inch and larger model or those featuring open framework wing structures.

A whole book could be written about covering and finishing techniques, but the limited scope of this publication will require that only the briefest of outlines of each method be given.

Tissue and nylon, with cellulose dope

The basic necessity here is to give the airframe two thorough coats of clear dope, thinned about 50/50 with thinners. It should then be rubbed down carefully. (NOTE: if the model has a foam/veneered wing, then great care must be taken to ensure that the surface of the wing is completely sealed before applying any cellulose to it; if the dope comes in contact with the foam, it will dissolve this.)

The covering medium is cut to size for each separate panel, and at this point the techniques for tissue and nylon differ slightly. For tissue covering, the pre-cut piece to be applied is then drawn across the surface of a tray of water to wet one side only. The material is placed wet side down on the airframe and 'painted' into place using plain thinners. The thinners will penetrate the tissue, dissolve the dope on the airframe and bond the covering in place. The edges of the covering are cut to a small (usually about ¼ inch) overlap and then this is doped over the edge. Where curves are involved, such as at wingtips etc, it will be necessary to nick the overlap with a number of small cuts in order to get it to dope smoothly around the edge—tissue will not conform to compound curves. When the thinners and water dry out, the tissue will tighten nicely. If some white marks ('blushing') appear at this stage, there is no need to worry as these will disappear upon application of the first coat of dope.

When using nylon, the pre-cut piece of covering material is thoroughly soaked with water under the tap, and then squeezed out before it is opened up and laid onto the surface. Once again it is 'painted' into place, but this time a mixture of thinned dope is used rather than pure thinners—about 40/60 dope/thinners is right. It may be de-

sirable to anchor one end of the material to the airframe (at the wing root, or nose of the fuselage) with a number of pins to prevent it 'creeping' as tension is applied. Unlike tissue, nylon can be persuaded to follow compound curves with care, so that areas such as wingtips and fuselage noses may be neatly covered with a little patience. Indeed, if the corners of a fuselage are well rounded, it is even possible to cover the complete structure with one piece of nylon, joining it along the bottom centre line of the fuselage—but this requires a certain amount of skill and patience, and the beginner would be better advised to use separate panels.

Whichever covering medium is being used, once the water has dried completely out, doping may commence. The secret here is to first of all dope around the edges to make absolutely sure that these areas are firmly fixed, and only commence general doping after this first coat has dried. Avoid using dope which is too thick; if your dope has been purchased from the model shop in small quarter or half litre tins, it should be diluted 50/50 with cellulose thinners. If you have obtained one of the five litre tins which can sometimes be obtained direct from the manufacturer (only worthwhile if you are going to be doing a good deal of building), you will find that this is much thicker and a dilution of 30% dope 70% thinners will be more appropriate. On the subject of thinners, this can be bought in five litre tins from most car accessory shops. Two words of caution, though; be absolutely sure to get *cellulose* thinners, *not* acrylic, and buy the more expensive variety, intended for use in spraying, rather than the cheaper type principally intended for spray-gun cleaning and other general uses.

The number of coats of dope required will vary widely. If the tissue or nylon is applied over a solid surface such as a foam/veneer wing or balsa sheet fuselage, then the aim is to apply sufficient to give a water resistant, smooth finish. On an open wing framework, however, the covering material must also be air-proofed if the wing is to be efficient. To achieve this will take anything from three coats of thinned dope on light-weight tissue to as many as eight on nylon. Gently rubbing down the surface, especially the edges, with *very fine* glass paper after the third or fourth and each subsequent coat helps in producing a nice finish.

Heat-shrink film and fabric

The best advice I can give here is 'follow the manufacturer's recommendations'. The minimum equipment you will need is an electric iron of some sort; it is perfectly possible to manage the whole job with just a lightweight domestic iron, but the availability of a heat-gun and/or special 'tacking' iron does make things easier.

Carry out a few experiments first with scraps of film to establish the required temperature settings for your particular iron—too hot and the film will 'shrivel', too cold and it will not adhere or shrink properly.

Cut the film or fabric to size allowing a reasonable overlap all round. Strip off the backing polythene sheet, and apply the panel, adhesive side down, to the airframe. Tack the material in place at one end of the panel with the iron. Now tension it gently in the longest direction, and tack the other end in place.

If the covering is being applied to a solid surface, it is necessary to start ironing the covering down along the mid-point, and then work outwards to the edges, if trapped air bubbles are to be avoided. If you do get a bubble, prick it with a pin and carefully work it down

with the iron. If an open frame wing is being covered, the film or fabric can be gently tensioned to the leading and trailing edges, tacked in place all the way around, and then shrunk tight.

The edges are trimmed to about ¼ inch overlap and ironed down firmly. When covering the adjoining panel, it is as well to note that film in particular does not adhere too well to itself; it may appear to give a good bond but the edges often work loose in use. A coat of varnish or fuel proofer along the joint is a good insurance against this problem.

Colour finish and decorating

More than any other subject, this is very much up to individual preference, but a few suggestions may be welcome.

Use the colour possibilities of the base covering material and avoid large quantities of coloured paint. Paint weight is purely parasitic, and while expenditure of extra weight in streng-thened structure is often worthwhile, parasitic weight is always to be avoided. Painted surfaces are also more difficult to repair.

Keep the colour scheme simple; a neatly executed scheme with flying surfaces of one colour and fuselage of another looks far better then a messy bestriped and checked affair.

Choose strong colours—red, orange, black, dark blue—and avoid wishy-washy pastels and (except as a trim line) white. Strong colours considerably aid visibility.

Avoid small areas of various colours—at a distance, especially against the type of background found at many slope soaring sites, these act like camouflage and cause the model to 'disappear'.

Finally . . . on the subject of construction. Care will always be repaid in the performance and the durability of the model. Once over the damaging learning stages, R/C model gliders, not being subjected to the constant vibration and attack from fuel seepage of their powered cousins, can last a very long time. There are many models being flown in my club which are well into their second *decade* of useful life.

It follows, therefore, that it is well worthwhile to take the time during construction to get the essentials—the fit of the important parts, the radio installation and the general accuracy of the airframe—right. If a joint you have just made is not quite right—undo it and remake it. If a part does not quite fit properly—modify it or make another. Time spent at this stage will be repaid many times over in trouble-free flying hours and resistance to damage in mishaps. After forty years of aero-modelling, I *still* have to keep reminding myself of these basic truths in order to achieve a high standard. As a clubmate once remarked; 'The only thing String-well can make in a hurry is a mess!'

Chapter 5
Basic slope flying

SINCE A GLIDER of any kind—radio controlled or free-flight, model or full-size—is, by definition, an aircraft without any form of on-board motive power, it is only able to descend through the air around it, trading off the potential energy bestowed by its initial height above the ground into the kenetic energy of its speed through the air. The efficiency with which it makes this transition can never be 100 percent of course, and is measured by a number of factors, principal among them being the glide angle, or the distance it can cover from a given height.

In order to prolong and sustain flight, and for the aircraft to actually gain height in relation to the ground, the air mass in which it is flying must be rising at a speed greater than the sinking speed of the aircraft—the glider must be 'in lift'.

There are, in general, two sources of such rising air; thermal lift which is considered later, and which may be found anywhere, and slope lift, which is associated with a hill or slope facing into a wind. The way in which slope lift is generated is illustrated by the sketch in Fig. 5.1. As the air is forced to rise over the slope an upward lift component is created, and it is this which the slope soaring radio controlled model uses to remain airborne. Naturally, the strength and extent of the lift generated varies in direct relation to a number of factors; the height and angle of the slope, the strength of the wind, whether or not it is blowing exactly at 90 degrees to the slope, the type of ground cover on the

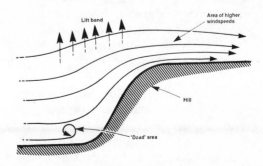

Fig. 5.1 Slope lift generation.

hill face (i.e. scrub, trees), and the topography in the area upwind of the slope.

The ideal slope would have a face angle of between 45 and 60 degrees, a smoothly rounded lip with a generous flat area behind, be covered in short grass and face out onto a flat area of land with no significant obstructions for ten miles or so, or onto the sea. While such 'ideal' slopes do exist (the best one I know is in the Isle of Man) and can produce truly amazing lift conditions, the vast majority of hills used by the modeller will have some shortcoming or other—shallower than the ideal, or steeper with a sharp 'lip' which causes turbulence, covered in trees, scrub or bushes, possessing a small, difficult (or in some cases) non-existent landing area, or suffering from other hills upwind which affect the lift. Far from upsetting the dedicated slope soarer, such problems are often regarded as challenges which make the hill more 'interesting' to fly!

From the beginners' point of view, a hill with a reasonably easy landing area, a sensible slope angle (30 to 60 degrees) and a fairly clear upwind area to reduce turbulence is to be desired. The time to explore the more difficult and interesting sites which you will hear about is when complete mastery of flying technique has been obtained. In identifying a suitable hill and recognising appropriate conditions of wind strength and direction for the model to be flown, the help of experienced local slope glider fliers is invaluable. Quite apart from the purely technical problems of choosing the correct slope, the matters of land ownership, access, permission to fly and any special local conditions (for example, some slopes are 'off limits' during lambing season) must be considered; usually local groups will have been through all the appropriate channels on these matters already.

Although it is not possible to describe all the variations of slope which the new glider guider may encounter, the following descriptions will give some idea of the principal possible variations, and their good and bad points.

'Ideal' site.—Fig. 5.2.

A ridge of reasonable length, with a slope angle of around 45 degrees and a smooth lip running out into a flat landing area behind.

'Normal' ridge—Fig. 5.3

Here the ridge falls away behind the crest, thus creating a lee slope which has considerable turbulence and down-draught over it.

Cliff—Fig. 5.4.

Steep or near-vertical slope with an abrupt edge and flat area behind. The lift area will be similar to the normal ridge in position, but generally narrower and more powerful. Severe turbulence will be encountered for some distance behind the edge.

Bowl—Fig. 5.5

This is a useful site in that it is capable of accepting rather more in the way of variation of wind direction than a

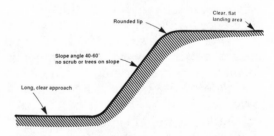

Fig. 5.2 'Ideal' slope site.

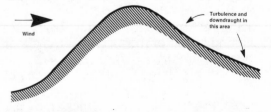

Fig. 5.3 'Normal' ridge.

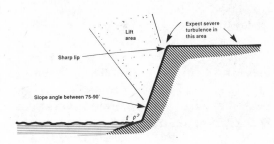

Fig. 5.4 Cliff.

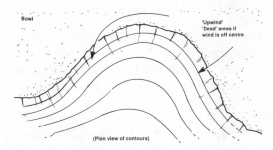

Fig. 5.5 Bowl.

straight ridge. However, if the wind is off centre, care is required to avoid the 'dead' area in the lee of the upwind arm of the bowl.

Naturally, many slopes are a combi-

A glorious slope soaring site with wonderful life—but only for the experienced; beginners should stick to safer hills.

nation of these basic types and, as stated above, ideal shapes and angles are rarely found. From the beginners' point of view, perhaps the most important consideration is the presence of a relatively flat and turbulence free landing area of reasonable size.

Preparation

Preparing a slope model for flight is no different from preparing any other radio controlled model. If possible get an experienced clubmate to cast an eye over the finished glider, this can head off a lot of problems. The balance point (often referred to as the centre of gravity or 'CG') should be in the position shown on the plan (often some ballast will be required in the nose to achieve this). For first flights, it may be an advantage to adjust the model so that it balances just a small distance in front of the CG position shown on the drawing. This will tend to make it a little more stable in the pitch or longitudinal sense, which can be an advantage in the early stages. However, this trick should not be overdone, otherwise it will want to fly in a permanent dive.

The wing (and tail, if it is removable) should be fixed firmly to the fuselage—if fastened by rubber bands, select ones which will be virtually at full stretch when fitted. In this way, the bands will exert sufficient pull to hold the wings properly in place (which is not the case if they are only partially stretched), and in the event of a crash they will snap, allowing the wings to break free with the minimum of damage.

All the control surfaces should be checked through their full range of movement to ensure that there is no tendency to bind or stick. Controls which are stiff or 'sticky' on the ground will often bind up completely in flight with the inevitable disastrous results. The linkages to the control surfaces should be adjusted to give the amount of movement specified by the plan or instructions. Here it is best to err on the side of a little more rudder movement than specified, but a little less elevator.

With the radio equipment switched on, the rudder and elevator should line up accurately with the fin and tailplane respectively, when the transmitter trim controls are in the central or neutral position. If they do not, adjust the screw-in clevises which connect the control rods to the surfaces until they do line up properly.

At this point, it will be worthwhile to try a test-glide with the model from a hand-launch on a suitable flat field. Have the radio switched on when doing this, but do not touch the controls unless you must to avoid a crash. Launch the model with the nose down at about 5 degrees, running forward and giving it a firm push rather than a hefty throw. The correct 'trim' to aim for with a slope soarer is a straight and steady descent, covering a distance of twenty or thirty yards from a six foot high launch.

If the model turns one way or the other, and there is no offset on the rudder, then either the wing or tail surfaces will probably be warped. In other words, the leading and trailing edge of the surface, as viewed from the front, will not be parallel. If, for example, the trailing edge of the right wingtip is warped down, relative to the leading edge (known as 'wash in'—trailing edge

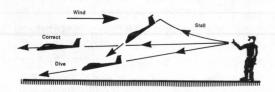

Fig. 5.6 Test gliding.

up warps, sometimes deliberately built-in both tips to aid stability, are called 'washout'), the model will turn to the left. This is easy to understand if you view the warp as acting like an aileron i.e. down aileron raises that wing. Warps are bad news, since their effect will vary with flying speed. Therefore, although the turn caused by a warp could be trimmed out with rudder offset during the hand gliding phase, once the model is launched from the hill and flown at a higher airspeed, its effect would reappear.

Every effort should be made to remove the warp by the gentle application of heat (an electric fire) or steam (a kettle) and twisting in the direction opposite to the warp. If, as may be the case with a very rigid foam wing, it is not possible to remove the warp, then it should be corrected by fixing an aluminium sheet tab to the trailing edge of the affected wing and bending this to counteract the effect of the warp (i.e. bent up to counteract wash in and down to offset washout).

Assuming that the glide from a hand-launch is now straight, the other factor to examine is the glide angle. If this is steeper than would be ideal, i.e. the model is tending to dive, then a little ballast should be removed from the nose until it improves. On the other hand, any tendency of the model to 'float' nose-up from a hand-launch is definitely to be avoided in a slope soarer, ballast should be added to the nose to correct this.

Once a satisfactory glide has been obtained, the controls can be tried *gently* during further hand glides, but a word of caution is in order here. It is very easy to stall the model, or turn it too tightly; at low altitude there will be no time to recover and a damaging crash will result. If a very gentle slope can be found, dropping away at an angle of four or five degrees only, then extended test glides can be made down this to explore the effects of gentle control movements. If the beginner is absolutely forced, due to geographical isolation, to attempt to teach himself to fly, this is the best way to start, since throwing the model off a 'real' hill without prior experience or some form of assistance is almost certain to lead to it crashing.

Progressing to the actual moment of flying, the following comments are made in the expectation that some form of experienced help will be available. It is worth re-stressing that the chances of an absolute novice successfully flying and landing a slope soarer entirely unaided are very slim.

A factor which must be considered is the natural flying speed of the model. All models, properly trimmed, will have a natural flying speed—say 15 miles per hour, which is probably typical for a trainer-type slope soaring model. If the wind speed on the day chosen for flying is greater than fifteen miles per hour, then the only way for the model to make progress into wind—away from the ridge—is by increasing its flying speed to a greater figure. This can be achieved in two ways—the most obvious is to give down elevator which will cause the model to dive and hence fly at a greater airspeed. This solution is often acceptable in slope soaring, since the constant hill lift is strong enough to still permit the model to climb relative to the ground although it is being dived through the rising air in order to 'penetrate' upwind.

A more sophisticated solution is to raise the model's wing loading by adding ballast in such a way that the balance point of the model remains unchanged, i.e. adding it around the CG position. As the wing loading is raised, so the model's natural flying speed will gradually increase. This is a useful trick, since although the glide angle of the model is steeper at the higher wing loading, it will still tend to fly more efficiently than a light model using a lot of down elevator, and will hence need less lift to sustain it.

On the whole, the beginner should avoid flying in conditions which are too windy for the natural penetration speed of his model, just as he should avoid flying in conditions of poor lift.

The main thing to remember is that one cannot simply pull in up elevator and climb as would be the case with a power driven model—you must have rising air. A common saying among glider fliers is that, if the model is descending, down elevator makes it descend faster while on the other hand up elevator also makes it descend faster, albeit in a nose-up attitude! In other words, the model will lose flying speed, stall (i.e. the wing will stop lifting) and fall out of the sky if too much up elevator is pulled in.

To take an early flight from start to finish:

Always launch the model nose down and give it a good firm throw. Remember that you will be (hopefully) launching into a stream of rising air, so unless the nose is held down the model will tend to balloon upwards and stall straight from the launch. Until proficient it is far better to have someone launch the model for you, so that you can be already in full control of the sticks from the moment of launch. The airflow on the edge of a slope can do strange things to a model (I have had one rolled inverted as it left the launcher's hand before you could say 'wreckage'—good for the adrenalin but bad for the bank balance!), so the aim is to punch straight out away from the hill as quickly as possible.

The cardinal rules for the beginner are:

Keep away from the ridge
Do not make 360 degree turns, keep 'essing' the model left and then right. Never, never, turn directly downwind towards the ridge until you are able to fly properly

For rudder/elevator models the turn should be initiated by a fairly big 'kick' of rudder, which is rapidly eased off and the model 'caught' with opposite rudder before it has turned more than 45 degrees. Forget about co-ordinating rudder and elevator in the earliest stages of learning to fly, this will come later. At first, use them separately; a gentle application of 'down' to increase speed slightly, followed by the big rudder kick to start the turn, a little 'up' to help it along, then opposite rudder to stop the turn and a little 'down' to stop the model from zooming as it exits the turn. Gradually, with experience, these movements will merge into a series of smooth and largely simultaneous control inputs, but this will take time. At first it is far easier to make a series of jerky stick movements, returning to neutral between each.

Should the model start to sink lower, guard against the dreaded 'up elevator' syndrome—keep the model flying at a reasonable speed and try to move it a little closer to the ridge until the lift improves again. Until you can really recognise lift, and make a fair assessment as to whether a patch of sinking air is likely to be of long or short duration, if in doubt it is always best to land—it can save you a long climb down the hill and back

As experience is gained, you will find that the easiest way to fly is to tack across the slope, with the model facing at an angle to the wind, holding in a little

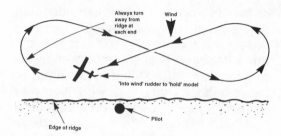

Fig. 5.7 'Tacking' along ridge.

'into wind' rudder and allowing the glider to proceed in a crab-like fashion.

Once you have mastery of the model, it is possible to fly for as long as the wind blows, or as long as the batteries last...but sooner or later comes the manoeuvre which has to be performed once each flight—the landing. I would assess the chances of a beginner launching and flying his first slope soarer successfully unaided as about 200 to 1 against; on the same scale, the chances of him landing it unaided without damage might be 5000 to 1! In other words, it is not easy!

Consider the problems for a moment; even on slopes with a 'good' landing area, there is likely to be some turbulence present, which you will not see until the model hits it, which, allowing for the relatively slow reactions of the beginner, will be far too late. The ground will probably be rough, with concealed rocks and pot holes, the wind gradient (i.e. the rate at which the wind speed increases with height above the ground) will be unpredictable and variable compared with flat ground and there will probably be more wind blowing than would be the case when undertaking first thermal soaring flights. Add to these factors the fact that a mighty sink will be waiting over the back of the hill, and it is easy to appreciate that, even for experienced slope soaring pilots, landings can sometimes be rather a lottery.

When learning to land your slope

soarer, do not attempt to fly a conventional 'circuit' approach as you would with a power model or thermal glider. If you do, one of two things will probably happen; the model will fly into the hill on the downwind leg, or, after turning into wind for the final approach, it will disappear smartly backwards (and downwards!) over the back of the hill. Instead try 'essing' back and forth, alternately to left and right, letting the model gradually drift back until it is over the landing area, and then applying down to fly it positively in to land. In this way, if the model is too high, it can simply be allowed to fly out into the lift again for another try, if too low it will undershoot, but hopefully not too seriously. The final thing to remember is that, on a windy hill, a classic 'power model' flare out, a foot above the ground, will lead to the model shooting up in the air and stalling in from six or seven feet, which can be very damaging. Resist the temptation to apply up elevator at the last moment, the model should be landed firmly, or 'flown on'.

Once the early flights (or as they were referred to more appropriately by a clubmate of mine, 'early frights!') are over, the beginner should fairly soon be able to cope with the model when it is away from the ridge and soaring in the lift area. However, he will still need help in the occasional 'difficult situation' which will arise, and also, for some time, with landings. Once extended periods of flying can be undertaken without constant rescue by the instructor, the novice should concentrate on extending his abilities by attempting to fly a pre-planned pattern—for example ten legs up and down the slope with 180 degree turns at each end, or a series of 270 degree turns whilst well out in the lift etc. The aim is to build up experience and confidence so that reactions to the model's attitude become automatic responses rather than each requiring a separate conscious decision. For this reason, more benefit can be obtained by carrying out pre-planned manoeuvres than by flying around aimlessly; in the latter situation the model often finishes up by going where *it* wishes to go rather than where the pilot wants it to be.

The next stage of development should see the pilot deliberately practising landings (horrifying as the thought of actually indulging in this awful task more often than strictly necessary may seem), since until he has mastered the difficult art of the 'slope side' landing, the number of sites on which he can fly will be severely limited to only those with a relatively flat landing area.

In essence, the slope side, or slope edge, landing is simplicity itself—it is all a matter of timing and using the airflow over the hill to advantage. The first time the novice sees an expert perform such a landing, he will be horrified; it looks awfully difficult. However, the problem can be approached in stages, which makes learning the technique fairly easy.

The aim is to place the model just above the ground as it slides out of an into-wind turn, in the area of maximum airflow just over the edge of the slope. In this way, the high wind speed reduces the ground speed of the model to zero, and it can then be gently 'plonked' down through the last couple of feet with down elevator, arriving with practically no forward speed. To be fair, this technique is actually easier with an aileron-equipped aerobatic model, but once learnt with a rudder elevator model, it will never be forgotten.

The technique is as follows:

Position the model out to left or right, about fifty yards away, above the edge of the ridge and about fifty feet up. Ease in down elevator and allow speed to build up as the model is dived down the slope. When the model is well out and below slope level, turn and fly across the slope for seventy or eighty yards, then turn directly towards the slope. The model, with excess speed, should now climb up the lift, climbing at the same angle as the slope (adjust the angle with the elevator). As the model approaches the slope, its speed decaying with the climb, start to skid it round in a turn; the aim is to complete the turn as the model arrives at the slope edge, so that it is facing into wind. At this point, faced by the maximum airflow just above the slope, the model's ground speed will be at its lowest and it can be neatly 'sat down' with little or no forward speed.

Needless to say, if this manoeuvre is carried out too low, the glider will hit the slope with a mighty crash while still travelling downwind. Too high, and it will simply slide forward and out into the lift again. The aim, then, is to work up to the finished article gradually, starting deliberately too high and making each subsequent attempt just a little lower until one is just right. The necessary judgement, which needs varying to suit the hill, model and wind conditions, will

be acquired surprisingly quickly and, like most flying, the whole procedure will soon become automatic. Trust me!

Once the new slope pilot can competently control his model from launch to landing, it is simply a matter of building up some air time to sharpen and refine his flying skills with the rudder/elevator trainer before progressing to an aileron model which will be capable of more advanced manoeuvres, as described later. After this, it is likely that the modeller will either build more, and hopefully better, aerobatic slope models, or will progress into pylon racing, cross-country or scale. Many slope soarers happily fly the same model for season after season, going out and enjoying themselves on their local hills in all conditions, without any thoughts of contest flying or building super scale models. This is indeed one of the attractions of radio glider flying in general and slope soaring in particular— it can be anything from a pleasant way to pass a few hours at the weekend in the open air and congenial company all the way to an all-consuming passion which excludes (almost!) all other spare time activities.

Chapter 6
Basic thermal flying

THE INITIAL stages of preparing a thermal soaring model for flight do not differ from those applied to a slope soarer as described in the previous chapter. However, since most thermal models are larger, and perhaps use less rigid structures, the need for checking the flying surfaces to ensure that they are warp-free should be re-emphasised.

When adjusting the balance of the model to locate the CG in the correct position, in this case stick strictly to the location shown on the plan. The other item which requires attention is the position of the tow hook. For safety, on initial flights, this should be located a little way in front of the CG position—half to one inch is typical. Later, when greater experience is gained, it will be found that better launches can be obtained by moving the hook rearwards so that it is on, or in some cases even behind the CG. However, this does make the model more prone to veering about on the towline, especially if line tension is low, so the more forward

position is best for the newcomer.

Since the thermal model is more likely to feature wings in two separate parts, plugged onto the fuselage via joining rods, very great care should have been taken at the assembly stage to ensure that both wings are at exactly the same angle to the fuselage datum line—the same 'incidence'. This is a problem point on many thermal soarers assembled by novice builders, and a model with wings at differing incidence angles is very difficult to fly accurately.

For initial test gliding, choose a calm day, or one with a very light breeze. The model should be hand-glided in exactly the same way as a slope soarer; however, as compared with a slope trainer model one would expect a two metre or 100 inch thermal soarer to cover 40 yards or more from a six foot launch, and the glide path appear much more 'floaty' than is the case with the more heavily loaded slope model. The same strictures regarding adjustment of the balance

Fig. 6.1 Hand tow launching.

point by small increments until the glide is a smooth descent, just below the stall, apply. At this point there is nothing further to be gained from hand gliding, all fine adjustments to the trim of the model require that it be launched to a reasonable height. In general, since a thermal soarer will normally be operating over flat fields away from the turbulence of the hills, the trim can be taken to much finer limits than is the case with the slope model; indeed, to achieve really satisfying soaring performances, the model must be quite precisely adjusted.

Coming to the launch itself, three methods are generally available, if we ignore power winches and aero-tow by power model, which are considered to be outside the scope of this book.

The simplest method is to use a hand tow-line, (see Fig. 6.1) which is stored on a winch. The winch is used merely to wind the line in after use, it is in no way involved in 'pulling' the model during the launch. The standard hand tow-line used by thermal soarers is 150 metres long, and is made of nylon monofilament fishing line. The model end carries a ring to engage with the tow hook, and just below this is a nylon pennant which serves both to pull the line free of the model at the top of the launch and give a visible indication to the timekeeper when the line is detached.

Line of 50 or 60 pounds breaking strain should be adequate for a normal 100S or two metre model, much heavier lines are used for the fast launching and heavy open models in competitions.

For your first flights, you should have

an experienced tow man—otherwise, you may well damage the model due to either towing too fast, or too slow! The technique is to lay the line out fully with the model directly downwind from the tow man. At a pre-arranged signal, the launcher holds the model overhead, with the nose about 20 degrees above the horizontal and the line attached to the tow hook. The tow man then runs away from the launcher, who, only when a reasonable pull of 15 to 20 pounds has built up as the nylon line stretches, releases the model by pushing it upwards and forwards *not* throwing it. The model will then climb like a kite, and the job of the tow man (which is why he needs to be experienced) is to keep a constant, safe tension on the line by running or walking, standing still or moving towards the model, as is necessary. Once the model reaches the top of the line, a gentle application of down elevator will enable it to be flown off.

It is not always possible to have a tow man available, and the so-called 'bungee' line, which is really a weak catapult, is used for single handed flying. This is composed of 20 percent rubber and 80 percent towline (see Fig. 6.2). In use, the anchor point is directly upwind of the launch point. After hooking on the line to the tow hook, the launcher walks downwind to stretch the rubber, usually about sixty or seventy metres. The model is then launched in exactly the same way as described above, and the gentle but firm pull of the rubber enables it to be kited up to close to the top of the line. In lighter winds there is inevitably more sag in a bungee line than would be experienced with the lighter hand tow-line, and in very calm conditions, it may not be possible to get a satisfactory launch.

When it is calm, my own club tends to favour use of the double return pulley

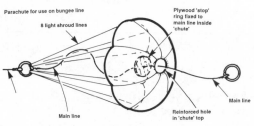

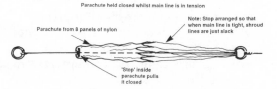

Fig. 6.2 'Bungee' line.

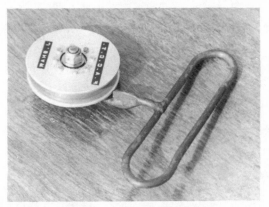

Hand-held pulley used in one of the methods of line launching described in the book.

launch, illustrated in Fig. 6.3. The advantage of this is that very little physical effort is required on the part of the tow man; also, he is close by the launcher and pilot rather than 150 metres away, which makes communication easier. Once again, however, an experienced hand is required on the towing pulley, since, with the built-in mechanical advantage, it is very easy to put rather too much strain on the model.

Once the model is free from the tow-line, flying a thermal soarer, providing that the model is properly adjusted, is

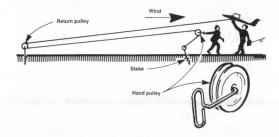

Fig. 6.3 Double return pulley launch.

just about the easiest kind of radio controlled flying possible. (This is not to imply that thermal soaring—as opposed to merely flying the model—is easy; a lot of skill and experience is required to progress from the stage of launching and gliding down to that of consistently finding rising air and making long flights.)

As with slope flying the novice should use the rudder and elevator controls separately at first. Turns can very quickly develop into spiral dives, so initially, if you want to turn through 360 degrees, make four separate 90 degree turns, with short legs in between to enable the model to settle down properly again. Fig. 6.4 illustrates the sequence in making this type of turn. Once again, the separate movements will, with experience, merge into one smooth sequence, so that continuous 'thermal turns' can be smoothly flown to enable the model to climb away in a thermal.

Landing is not as difficult as on the slope, since a proper approach may be flown. However, the biggest single problem which the beginner must overcome, and the one which causes most crashes, is that of 'visually reversed' controls. When the model and pilot are facing the same way there is no problem—left stick gives left rudder

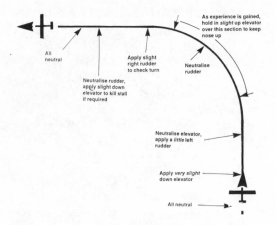

Fig. 6.4 Turns.

and vice versa. However, since we are not actually sitting in the model, if the aircraft is flying towards the pilot (as it would normally be during the last stages of a landing approach) a model turning to the pilot's *right* requires left rudder to correct it—which is very definitely not a natural reaction.

If a 'normal' landing approach, as illustrated by Fig. 6.5 is made, this problem of reversed control will occur during the final leg, and can easily lead to a crash. Until the proper control response becomes automatic (once again, a matter of flying time and practice), there are a couple of 'tricks' which help when the model is flying towards the pilot. One is to repeat (out loud, if you don't mind the candid comments from clubmates) 'if it's going left, give it left'. The other, less public, is

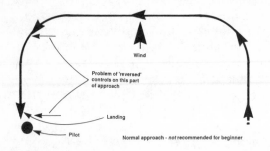

Fig. 6.5 'Normal' landing approach.

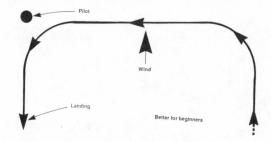

Fig. 6.6 Beginner's landing approach.

to always 'put the (transmitter) stick under the low wing'.

However, as far as the landing is concerned, it is better in the early stages to avoid the problem altogether by making the approach as in Fig. 6.6.

Another major problem in early flights, since the thermal model is necessarily trimmed fairly near the stall, will be the 'increasing' stall. What happens here is that, perhaps by over application of up elevator, or by failing to kill the slight zoom as the model leaves a turn , it stalls. Any well trimmed model, left to its own devices, would normally settle down after one or two oscillations—but instead the stall gets worse and worse, and, unless something is done, finishes with a large thump into the ground. What is actually happening is that the novice pilot's corrective actions are being applied too late—up elevator after it has begun the climb up to the stall, and down after it has actually popped over the top.

If the stall is slight, rather than pumping the elevator stick, wait until the model is nearly at the bottom of a swoop and, just before the nose starts to rise, apply a little rudder. This will 'turn the model off the stall' quite neatly. For a more severe stall, it is necessary to ease in down elevator just as the model is about to start climbing after the swoop down, as illustrated by Fig. 6.7.

In the initial stages, the beginner should not worry about spot landings or

Apply slight down
elevator here

Fig. 6.7 Killing a stall.

duration of flight; the sole aim should be a safe launch followed by a smooth fly around and a safe landing somewhere within the field—better a hundred yards walk to a whole model than a five yard one to a heap of pieces! Avoid making turns low down, set your landing approach up with plenty of height in hand then just concentrate upon keeping it straight and level until touchdown.

Chapter 7
Basic slope aerobatics

ONCE THE newcomer has achieved that happy state where he can fly his slope soarer in a variety of lift conditions and land it safely, his thoughts are almost certain to turn to the subject of aerobatics. The trainer model which has served him so well through the learning phase will perform a very limited range of aerobatics; usually loops and stall turns and spins are easily within the scope of such a model, indeed, because of their directional stability it is often easier to perform good loops with a rudder/ elevator trainer than with a 'genuine' aerobatic aileron model. Roll off the top, barrel rolls, spins and some limited inverted flying can also often be performed with such a model, but these latter manoeuvres are not particularly easy, nor very satisfactory in appearance.

The key to aerobatic performance is the ability to fly and soar in the inverted position. Inverted performance in a power model is easy to achieve—simply fit a wing with a section having equal camber on top and bottom (a 'symmetrical' section) and apply a big enough motor to the front end. A glider, however, is reliant upon the energy it can derive from its ability to turn rising air into height gained, which can then be traded off into speed. In this respect, symmetrical sections are not very effi-

Lightweight 'V' tail 'fun' slope soarer zips past the camera; this is the R.M. 'Veedette' prototype, my own design.

cient, and although many slope aero-batic models do use such a section, they require good lift to perform to their best advantage. The alternative approach is to use a 'semi-symmetrical' section, such as Eppler 374; this will not be so efficient when upside down, but is a much better soaring section. Hence the greater height gained can be turned into more speed to give better aerobatics, and the performances produced by the two approaches in the right hands are very similar.

Aerobatics using 'proper' aerobatic (aileron) soarers are dealt with later, this chapter is concerned principally with exploring those first manoeuvres carried out after flying competence has been attained.

First of all a word about positioning of aerobatics. Since the slope soarer is flying in a constant wind which is blowing towards the hill, and which is travelling at greater velocity over the top of the ridge, some care is required. The model will drift back towards the hill during aerobatics, so initially all man-oeuvres should be started well out from the ridge and with adequate height in hand. The time for close-in, tight, aerobatic flying is when you are really proficient, and probably not with this model!

The simplest of all aerobatics is the loop. Position the model slightly off to one side and fly it straight upwind out from the ridge. When about 100 yards

upwind, ease in down elevator and enter a gentle dive. Sustain the dive whilst some excess speed builds up and then neutralise and pull in half to two thirds up elevator. The model will climb up, and if you have sufficient speed, it will continue over the top of the loop. Ease off the up elevator as the model descends around the back of the loop, and as it reaches the bottom apply a little down to stop it zooming up again and recover into level flight.

Once single loops are mastered, try consecutive ones. The secret here is to ease right off the up as the model comes around the back of the loop to let it build up a little more speed and then, instead of applying down, revert to up elevator as it passes through level flight at the bottom. Watch out for the drift back into the hill.

For best effect, loops should really be performed cross-wind, parallel to the slope. This is much more difficult, especially with a rudder/elevator model, as the cross-wind will push the model towards the slope and tend to make it 'screw' out of the loop. To be able to perform three good, superimposed loops cross-wind requires a lot of practice.

Stall turns are easy if performed in the right direction, with the model turning into wind. Actually, if you can do stall turns with a rudder/elevator model, you will do really excellent ones later with an aileron model. This is because rudder on a flat-winged aileron model produces just *yaw* (the fuselage changing heading whilst the wings remain level) while, with the dihedral equipped rudder model, it produces *roll* as well (one wing drops). For the stall turn, yaw only is what we want, and to minimise the roll effect we do the manoeuvre cross-wind.

To do a stall turn to the right, approach from the right flying parallel to the ridge. Dive the model gently, allowing it to pick up similar speed to that required for a

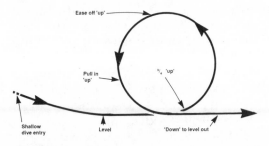

Fig. 7.1 The loop.

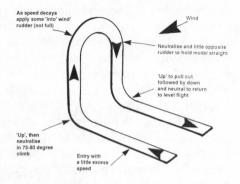

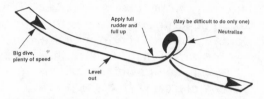

Fig. 7.4 Flick rolls.

Fig. 7.2 Stall turn.

loop. Neutralise, and then pull in up elevator until the model is climbing at about 60 degrees to the horizontal. Ease off the up elevator to hold it in the climb, and as the speed decays, at the point when it is travelling just slower than normal flying speed, apply a quick 'kick' of right rudder. When timed just right the model will remain flat but rotate through 180 degrees to dive back the way it came. Let speed build up and then pull out to level flight at the entry height with up and then down elevator.

To do a stall turn to the left, approach from the left. In actual fact, even without the application of rudder, a well balanced design will often carry out immaculate stall turns if flown like this, the wind pushes the tail around as flying speed is lost in the climb. Double stall turns, one to the left followed immediately by one to the right, look impressive.

Rolling manoeuvres are possible with rudder/elevator models, but tend to be of the 'barrel roll' or 'flick roll' variety. To perform a barrel roll, achieve rather

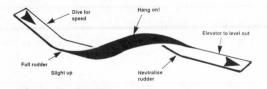

Fig. 7.3 Barrel roll.

more speed than for a loop, pull the model 10 degrees nose-up and then apply full rudder and hang on! The model should rotate as though passing round the outside of a barrel. Recover at the appropriate moment by releasing rudder and applying a little down elevator. Some models will flick roll (indeed, some do it when least expected!), although stable trainers may have wing washout built in to prevent this and inhibit spinning. You will need a fair amount of rudder and elevator movement, and do try this with good height and distance from the ridge in hand, as the outcome is often a little uncertain! Dive and allow a good excess of speed to build up. Level out and immediately apply full up elevator and full rudder one way. If too stable, the model will merely execute a sloppy barrel roll. On the other hand it might flick around in one or more rapid, almost axial, rolls. If the controls are held on too long in this case, the glider will probably fall into a spin, so release quickly to recover into level flight.

The spin itself is a pretty and easy manoeuvre which can be entered from level flight by gently easing in up elevator and, just as the model stalls, applying full up and full rudder one way. The model should drop into a spin in the direction of the applied rudder. To recover, wait until the model is passing through a direction 180 degrees away from the desired recovery track, release the controls and apply a 'kick' of opposite rudder followed by down elevator to recover into a straight dive. Do

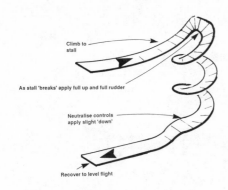

Climb to
stall

As stall 'breaks' apply full up and full rudder

Neutralise controls
apply slight 'down'

Recover to level flight

Fig. 7.5 Spin.

remember that a spinning model loses height rapidly, so start this one high until you are used to it (indeed, it is a safe way of descending if sucked up to great height by a passing thermal, without over-stressing the airframe).

There is a great deal of enjoyment to be had out of exploring the flight characteristics of even the most basic slope trainer, and a valid challenge in extracting maximum performance from these simple models. Always keep a look-out for other users of the hill when practising aerobatics, and think SAFETY.

Chapter 8
Basic thermal soaring

POSSIBLY MORE than any other branch of radio controlled glider flying, learning to recognise and use thermal lift to prolong flights is something which can only be really learned by practical 'hands on' experience.

As with slope aerobatics, the starting point is for the newcomer to have progressed to the stage of being able to confidently fly his model, putting it where he wants in the sky and landing it safely and close to the intended spot. Having reached this point, the next stage is to discover the magic of climbing the model away to great height in a thermal 'bubble' and returning it safely to the pilot's feet after a flight of 30, 40 or more minutes.

About thermals

First of all, the novice thermal pilot should stick to reasonable weather conditions. Lift can be found even on the most unpromising days, but it is easier when the winds are light and the sun is shining.

Secondly, it is necessary to appreciate something of the nature of the lift we are seeking to exploit. Unlike slope lift, the generation of which is easily understood, thermal lift is a more complex and less easily definable phenomenon. It is common knowledge that warm air rises, and this is the basis for all thermal lift. If a mass of air becomes warmer than the general air surrounding it, it will rise, cooling by expansion as it does so. However, since the average air temperature will decrease with altitude above the ground, some differential between the temperature of the mass of air in our 'thermal' and the surrounding air will be maintained and it will continue to rise until the two temperatures eventually coincide.

Since air can only be warmed by contact, thermal generation during the day is usually associated with areas of ground surface which are more efficient at reflecting heat—concrete and tarmac areas, large building roofs and short grass fields. Later in the evening, lift is generated from areas which are efficient 'heat stores'—woods, long grass areas etc. Naturally, once the warmed mass of air breaks free from the ground it will drift with the wind as it rises (see Fig. 8.1). It is this effect which makes thermal flying more difficult on windy days, since the length of time for which a model, piloted from a fixed ground location, can be kept in the rapidly drifting rising air is strictly limited by the operator's eyesight.

The topography of the surrounding area will have a considerable effect on thermal generation. Relatively small

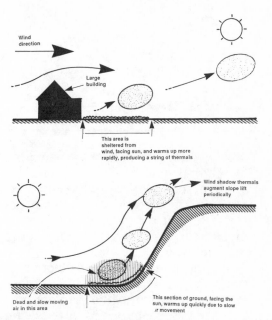

Fig. 8.2 (a) Wind shadow thermals. (b) Wind shadow thermal generation on a slope.

ground features, such as walls, lines of bushes etc. seem to 'trigger' lift patches into rising as the wind blows across them. Much more important, and widespread, though, is the 'wind shadow' effect. This simply means that if an area of ground upon which the sun is shining is protected by some feature from the wind—it is in the lee of a large building, row of trees or small ridge—it will heat up more rapidly and release a continuous stream of thermals (see Fig. 8.2). Incidentally, this factor is also important to slope soarers, since the area at the upwind base of a slope is an area of stagnant or slow moving air. Often, then, thermals are triggered in this area which then rise up to join the slope lift at the crest of the hill (see Fig. 8.3).

How to find lift

This is all well and good, but after spending a good few days seeking, and

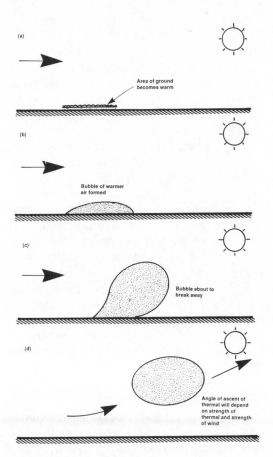

Fig. 8.1 Formation of thermal.

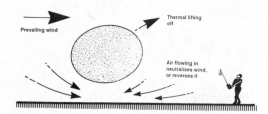

Fig. 8.3 Effect of thermal on prevailing wind.

probably failing to find, the elusive lift, the thermal novice may well become exasperated. As you cannot *see* lift, how can you tell where it is? Well, lift may not be visible, but the reaction of various other things to lift is visible, and there are many ways of detecting it.

First and foremost is the reaction of the pilot's own model. Did it tow more easily to the top of the line than normal? If so it was probably in lift. Is the normally stable model being bounced around by turbulence, despite the light wind? Lift always has turbulence associated with it around the edges, so here is a positive indicator. If one wing kicks up and the model enters a turn without any bidding from the transmitter, then try reversing the turn and 'flying into the rising wing'—something has caused the wing to kick up, probably lift.

Obviously, if other gliders are being flown at the same time, these should also be watched for similar symptoms. At the heights to which we launch (400 to 500 feet), lift patches are often very localised, so that one model can be climbing rapidly in lift whilst another as little as fifty or sixty yards away may be struggling around in sink.

Certain birds can be very useful lift markers. Gulls are an obvious indicator, it is very easy to tell by their stiff winged circling when they have contacted lift. Other birds such as rooks and crows also use lift on occasions, and closer to the ground, insect feeding birds such as swifts, swallows and martins provide useful indications. These birds do not

soar themselves, but they do feed on insects which are often sucked up by patches of rising air, and many times lift can be picked up almost from ground level by observing their behaviour.

Perhaps the best lift indicator of all, though, is the wind. In wind strengths up to light breezes, the behaviour of the wind, if observed carefully, can give an unerring pointer to the elusive thermal. When a thermal lifts off, the rising warm air is replaced by other air which flows in under it as shown in Fig. 8.3. If the prevailing wind blowing at the time is only light, this air movement will have a marked and easily perceptible effect upon it. For example, if the modeller suddenly feels the wind fall away, or in very light breezes, even reverse its direction, then there will be a thermal lifting off upwind of him (i.e. upwind in relation to the 'normal' wind direction blowing on that day). Conversely, if the wind strength increases, the thermal centre will be downwind. If it veers to blow from further to the right, the thermal is on the left and so on.

This 'wind shift' effect is amazingly consistent, and works time after time as a thermal detector. For this reason, you will see that most experienced thermal soaring pilots have a light streamer (knitting wool or something similar), on the end of their transmitter aerial, so that they can constantly monitor the wind direction whilst flying.

Free-flight contest modellers make much use of ultra-light Mylar streamers mounted on poles some 200 metres or more upwind of the launch area. These streamers normally blow out in the lightest breeze, but if a thermal passes over the area, they behave quite differently, often rising vertically in the air for their full length. Such aids as these can be useful to the radio control soaring pilot when sport flying. However, they are not much used in contests, since all the owner's opponents can also see and take advantage of them.

It is apparent then , that by observation of a range of factors, some relating to the model itself, others to the surrounding environment, the chances of contacting lift can be improved. It does take time for these observations, and the analysis of the data which they are providing, to become automatic. Until this degree of automatic response is attained, thermal soaring can be, mentally, quite hard work. There is absolutely no substitute for lots of practice flying, nor for having a model which is properly adjusted to fly straight and smoothly at its lowest sinking speed, without interference from the pilot. Many experienced thermal soaring pilots talk about the 'feel' of the model. Of course, there can be no direct feedback 'feel' on the transmitter, but, sooner or later, the newcomer will experience a flight which will make clear the use of the word 'feel' in this context. Sometimes the model just sits right in the air and 'feels' right—there is no other way to describe it. On these occasions one can be absolutely sure that it is in lift.

How to use it

Once some lift is detected, the priority must be to keep the model in it, and maximise the height gained from the lift while it is within flying range of the launch point. The normal way in which this is done is to circle the model and let it drift at windspeed. However, care is required since, in doing this, it is often possible to work the model out of the lift! The golden rule when circling in lift is to constantly observe the behaviour of the model. Unless you have been lucky enough (or skilful enough!) to find the central, strongest area of the lift patch

immediately, the odds are that one portion of the circle will show a better rate of climb than the rest. Favour this side by making the next circle 'egg-shaped' and then watch again. Keep moving the model in this way until the whole of the circle shows a uniform rate of climb, and you will have centred the lift (or, to quote the current American jargon 'cored out'!).

Sometimes, patches of lift will be contacted which do not seem to behave like a normal thermal in that they do not seem to drift downwind. In these circumstances, the pilot usually starts circling, only to find out after a few turns that the model has stopped climbing—it has 'fallen out' of the downwind edge of the lift patch. Under these circumstances, the correct action is to move back upwind to contact the lift and then, instead of circling, 'ess' the model back and forth, rather as you would when slope soaring. It is likely that lift patches such as this are really low-level wave lift, generated by ground features some distance (even miles) upwind of the flying site.

. . . then how to lose it!

Having found our lift, it is very easy for the novice to be literally carried away by it all, and find that the model has dwindled to a dot at great height and distance. Caution is required, since it is very difficult to accurately fly a model in these circumstances, and, if over course control movements are used, it is very easy to accidentally over-stress the airframe and pull off some vital component, like a wing for instance!

In the early stages always quit the thermal by flying away in a straight line while you still have comfortable visual contact with the model, i.e. while it is still recognisable *as* a model rather than appearing as a dot. If you *do* get too high, you will appreciate the importance of having a model which will fly itself. The main thing to remember is to heed the advice of *The Hitchhiker's Guide to the Galaxy* and *'don't panic'!* Ease in about half down trim, and then concentrate in keeping the model in a straight line coming towards you. Do not circle, and do not indulge in large movements of the elevator control. If the model has airbrakes, deploy them, and readjust the elevator trim into the position which has been previously established as the right one for flight with airbrakes out.

The best way to escape is to fly the model in long straight legs; in this way you will lose the lift and the model should fly itself with minimum interference. If there are other modellers present on the field, ask them to help keep track of the model until you get it down to a comfortable height again. If the sky is a mixture of cloud and blue, try to keep the model against a cloud background, it will be much easier to see.

To someone who has yet to experience their first really big thermal, the above advice may seem superfluous, but believe me, it is not; there have been many times in the past fifteen years when, notwithstanding excellent eyesight, I have very nearly lost visual contact with the model.

Golden rules

To revert from the art of losing lift to that of finding it here is a summary of some golden rules for finding and using thermals:

1 Be familiar with your flying site and the likely sources of thermals—car parks, buildings, wind shadow areas etc—around it.
2 Monitor the wind when flying and be alive to any changes in direction and strength which may point to lift.
3 Watch for soaring birds and also for insect feeders close to the ground.
4 Watch any other models flying in different parts of the sky from your own.
5 During lift searches, it is much easier to detect movements of the model if it is some distance away horizontally, rather than directly overhead.
6 Note the behaviour of the model during the tow-launch; if the rate of climb is faster than normal it is probably being towed through lift.
7 Watch for anything which disturbs the normal flight path of the model and always turn towards such disturbances. In particular, if a model trimmed to fly straight suddenly starts turning one way, turn it back and fly in the opposite direction.
8 Watch the 'sit' of the model during flight. If it speeds up and starts to 'bounce', lift is almost certainly there. On the other hand, if it suddenly requires more up elevator, and then starts to sink in a nose up attitude, rapid action is required to move away from the area since sink is indicated.

It is a fact that the newcomer to thermal soaring, even if experienced in other branches of radio flying, is likely to have a most frustrating time at first. He will fly through many usable patches of lift, simply not recognising them for what they are. There are few things more annoying than watching experienced thermal soarers on the same field winding their models away in lift time after time while you are simply going to the top of the tow-line and back to earth in five or six minutes. The best plan in these circumstances is to pick out the most consistently successful pilot, and when he has landed his model, ask him to 'spot' for you. Explain that, although you can fly the model you are having trouble in finding lift. Having asked for his help, do exactly what he says, and if he is a good thermal soaring pilot, the odds are he will put you in lift within the first few launches. After the flight, don't just thank him, but ask 'Why?' Why did he give you a particular instruction, what did he see that gave away the lift to him? Now relate the answers to the flight you have just had and try to do the same without his help.

It will take time, but the rewards in satisfaction gained from extending a dead air flying time of six minutes up to and beyond the hour mark with no more aid than the invisible air are very great, and worth the effort.

Chapter 9
Aileron models

UP TO NOW, the models we have discussed have used rudder and elevator as the sole flying controls. There are a number of reasons why I favour this approach for the novice. A wing with ailerons can require a good deal more constructional skill than one without, duration thermal soarers do not need ailerons to perform satisfactorily, whilst aileron slope soarers, unless specifically designed as trainers, tend to have flying characteristics more suited to the pilot with some experience. However, to become a 'complete' R/C pilot, experience with aileron-equipped models is desirable.

On the thermal soaring side, it is perfectly possible to become a very competent flier, even a top competitor, without ever flying an aileron model. However, it is increasingly being recognised that an aileron-equipped thermal soarer is very useful in certain conditions, and to this extent some aileron experience will stand in good stead even the modeller who intends to specialise in thermal soaring alone. This experience is best acquired with a slope soarer; if the pilot can fly an aerobatic aileron slope model, he will have absolutely no problems with the much 'softer' response of the aileron-equipped, essentially non-aerobatic, thermal soaring sailplane. Of course, if it is the beginner's ultimate aim to enter the world of scale sailplanes, then aileron experience is essential.

As implied above, aileron models come in different varieties; an 'adapted' slope trainer with an aileron wing will generally be a relatively stable model with a fairly limited aerobatic repertoire, ideal as a follow up to the modeller's first slope soarer. The genuine slope aerobatic model, with fully or semi-symmetrical wing section, little or no dihedral and large, powerful ailerons is not so easy, since, having little automatic stability, it needs to be flown all the time with constant control inputs but rewards its owner by being capable of any sort of aerobatics in the right circumstances. The large slope cross-country model, or aileron-equipped open class thermal soarer (typically these models will be anything between 10 and 15 feet in wingspan) uses ailerons to give greater precision of control in the rolling plane with these large spans. The aim is not to fly aerobatics, so some dihedral is incorporated in the design to give a degree of automatic stability and, once the modeller is used to them, these models are generally no more difficult to fly than a large rudder/elevator soarer, and in some respects (e.g. landing approaches in breezy conditions) actually easier.

The easiest way into aileron flying is to build an aileron wing for an existing slope trainer—if you have been very lucky your first model may have survived the rigours of the learning period in sufficiently good condition to be of use here! Such a wing can be of the same size and outline as the original, but should use approximately half the dihedral and, preferably, a wing section such as Eppler 374 which has some degree of camber on the underside, rather than the substantially flat-bottom section of the original trainer. Such a model as this will have a limited ability in the rolling plane, enabling practice of straightforward rolls, roll off the top and cuban eight (a loop with a half roll on the downward leg followed immediately by another loop and half roll to produce a horizontal figure eight with a 'knot' in the middle). The dihedral and layout will make it a stable and easy model to fly, but at the same time will detract from the rolling performance, so that after some experience with this type of model, the pilot will be ready to tackle the more difficult but rewarding fully aerobatic slope model.

A 'true' aerobatic slope soarer will have a wing which is virtually flat, large ailerons, and use a wing section which is either a combination of a semi-symmetrical type at the root changing to a fully symmetrical one at the tip, or is fully symmetrical overall. It will fly as well inverted as upright, and once the knack of flying such a model is mastered, 'up' and 'down' take on whole new meanings—the possibilities, given reasonable lift, being only limited by the pilot's skill, reflexes and nerve.

Since there is no external source of power, an aerobatic glider requires a hill which produces reasonably good lift to realise its true potential. This is not to say that they cannot be flown in more marginal conditions, but flying such a model when there is only enough lift to permit 'scratching' up and down along the ridge, with just the occasional hasty roll or loop thrown in, is like harnessing a Derby winner to a milk float! A larger, more lift-efficient semi-aerobatic model will give more satisfaction in such circumstances. Given decent lift, the art of performing good aerobatics on the slope can be summed up by the phrase 'conservation of energy'. In other words, the aim must be to keep the model moving smoothly at good speed all the time, avoid course control movements and sudden, drag-producing changes of direction and string the whole pattern together so that speed picked up on the exit from one manoeuvre can be used in the following one.

Generally speaking, aerobatics may be divided into three groups; those in the looping plane, those in the rolling plane and those combining looping and rolling. In addition, manoeuvres such as the stall turn use the fact that a flat wing aileron model will yaw sideways when rudder is applied to it, rather than bank.

Simplest of the rolling manoeuvres is the straightforward axial roll. For a single roll, dive across the slope, level out and immediately apply full aileron, releasing it when the model has almost

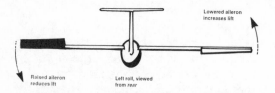

Fig. 9.1 Aileron turning.

completed its rotation. With most aero-batic models, a single roll, given sufficient flying speed, can be completed without the need to correct the flight path by the use of rudder during the portions of the roll when the model is on its side, and down elevator during the inverted portion. However, to perform consecutive rolls, progressive use of these corrections is necessary, and it requires a good deal of practice to perfect the technique.

Once the pilot has mastered consecutive fast axial rolls, the next challenge is the hesitation roll, which definitely does require the use of coordinated rudder and elevator inputs. This manoeuvre is best started with good speed, and involves snapping in full aileron and rapidly neutralising to hold the model on its side for a brief period after 90 degrees of roll have been completed, followed by a further 90 degrees and pause in the inverted position and so on. This is a four point roll. Much more difficult is the eight point roll where the roll is stopped every 45 degrees of rotation. If proper rudder and elevator corrections are not made, it is impossible to hold a hesitation roll on track, and the same comment applies to the next more difficult roll, the slow roll. Here only partial aileron is used to give a deliberately slow rate of rotation, the aim being that the model should cover a

large distance during the course of completing the roll. Naturally, this is more difficult than rolling quickly, since the glider immediately tries to deviate off track and has to be held on its heading with constantly changing rudder and elevator inputs, while holding a constant rate of roll. If this sounds difficult, that is because it *is* difficult!

Loops are performed as was earlier described for rudder/elevator models, although in consecutive loops subtle use of the ailerons may be needed to keep the wings level. Outside loops, sometimes called 'bunts', are performed with *down* elevator; if these are done downwards from level flight, a certain amount of nerve is required for the first attempts. It is probably easier to wait until inverted flight has been mastered and attempt the first outside loops upwards from inverted, just to prove that the model *will* go round safely in this direction.

Inverted flight, if the model is set up properly, is simply a matter of remembering that the elevator control is reversed, although aileron acts in the same direction as when upright. A common tendency to avoid when inverted is the temptation to pull the nose up too much and stall the model.

Spins, both upright and inverted, are quite straightforward, although some aerobatic models may require aileron throwing in at the appropriate moment as well as rudder to start them spinning.

The combination manoeuvres will follow naturally after the basics have been learned; performing them perfectly in the slope environment, with its constant wind and occasional turbulence is a challenge. Roll off the top (half

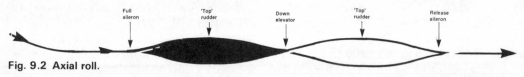

Fig. 9.2 Axial roll.

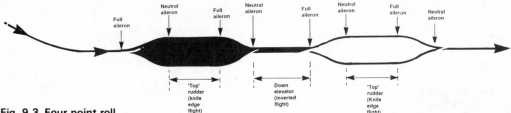

Fig. 9.3 Four point roll.

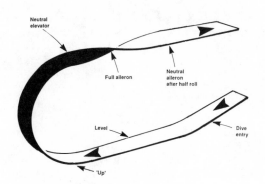

Fig. 9.4 Roll off the top.

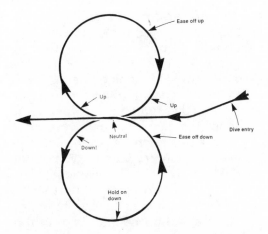

Fig. 9.5 Vertical eight.

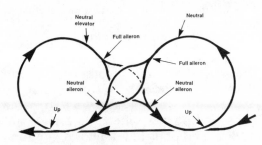

Fig. 9.6 Cuban eight.

inside loop, half roll) or off the bottom (half outside loop, half roll), horizontal and vertical eight (one inside and one outside loop), cuban eight (two inside loops and two half rolls) are fairly easy. Given enough speed, variations such as square and triangular loops and eights are possible, as are vertical rolls (up and down) and some figures which defy description!

It must be emphasised that to produce really recognisable figures requires a good model, the right conditions and a great deal of practice. The novice should not be disappointed if his first aerobatics are barely recognisable, it will take time to become really proficient, but the practising is most enjoyable, so why worry?

A final word on the process of adjusting an aerobatic slope model may be worthwhile. Once the model is flying reasonably well, the aim is to achieve 'neutral stability', so that, as far as is possible, the glider will stay in whatever attitude the controls place it until the next control input. To achieve this, put the model in a gentle dive across the slope, neutralise all controls and watch its reaction. If the dive becomes steeper, move the CG forward a touch and try again. If, on the other hand, the model pulls out of the dive on its own, move the CG back a touch and try again. These adjustments may, at first thought, seem contrary to what one would expect, but rest assured that they are correct. The aim is to produce a model which will hold the dive at a constant angle until it is pulled out with up elevator.

Chapter 10
Airbrakes and spoilers

THERE SEEMS to be something of a disagreement between slope and thermal soaring R/C pilots about the merits of fitting some form of airbrake or spoiler system to their models. The majority of thermal soaring models of 100 inches or greater span now feature brakes or spoilers; the very considerable lift generated by the large, efficient wings of such models makes them very difficult to land precisely without such aids. On the slope, with the exception of the large cross-country models and, naturally, scale sailplanes, brakes or spoilers are seldom seen. Certainly the much smaller and more agile slope models, both trainers and aerobatic types, are easier to land without the use of brakes. However, it may be significant that, if the slope enthusiast once operates a model with brakes, all his future productions tend to have them— they do make life much easier.

It would be as well to define the principal difference between airbrakes and spoilers. Spoilers act by destroying the lift generating capabilities of a portion of the wing; they will also, as a side effect, produce extra drag. Brakes, on the other hand, principally produce extra drag, any lift spoiling being a side effect. In practice either type works well on most models, with the airbrake being the most effective system for very clean and fast types such as pylon racers or slope cross-country models. With large area, comparatively lightly loaded, thermal soarers, the reverse applies since, to be effective, it is necessary to inhibit the lift production of the wing; in this case, a spoiler system works best.

Whether brakes or spoilers are used the critical points are that they should work reliably every time and, equally important, not cause a degradation in the performance of the model when they are not working. In other words, the engineering of the system must be carried out sufficiently well to avoid gaps and bumps when the brakes are closed, and poor fit leading to jamming and stickiness when they are operated.

For this reason, it is unlikely that the beginner would want to fit brakes or spoilers to his first or even second model, but after that they could be considered as necessary on thermal soaring types and optional, but desirable, on slope models.

Rather than enter into a long description of the very many alternative systems which are in use, reference to Figs. 10.1–10.5 will illustrate some of the more commonly encountered schemes. The most popular of these systems, the weighted blade top surface spoiler (Fig.

10.1) and the trailing edge brake (Fig. 10.4) are the ones I would recommend; the former for thermal models and the latter for either thermal or slope models. Of these systems, the weighted blade variety is perhaps the easiest to fit, with a simple system of actuation relying upon the servo pulling on a chord. However, the actual blades for this system need to be located around the point of maximum camber of the wing, which is perhaps the most important and sensitive area from a lift generation point of view. Hence great care needs to

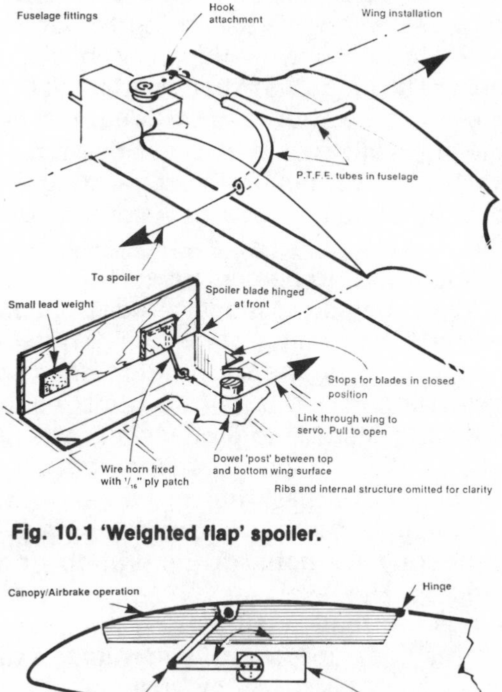

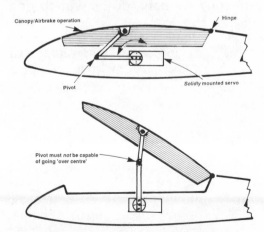

Fig. 10.1 'Weighted flap' spoiler.

Fig. 10.2 Fuselage canopy brake.

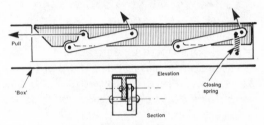

Fig. 10.3 Single action 'blade brakes'.

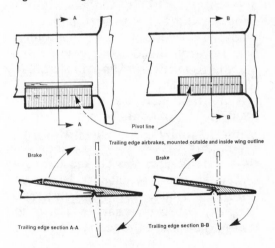

Fig. 10.4 Trailing edge brakes.

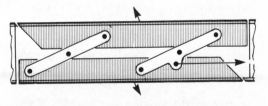

Fig. 10.5 Double action 'blade' brakes.

be taken to ensure a good fit of the blades if the efficiency of the wing is not to be impaired. Trailing edge brakes, while mechanically more complex to fit and actuate, are more forgiving in this respect.

Operationally, the newcomer will have to carry out quite a lot of flying to come completely to grips with the action of brakes or spoilers. It is difficult to generalise upon the reaction of any particular model, but mostly top surface blade spoilers will cause a nose down trim shift, while the reaction to trailing edge brakes will vary between no trim change at all and a nose up trim tendency. In terms of a landing approach, the normal technique with top surface spoilers is to ease in up elevator as the spoilers are opened so that the model will slow down and sink nose up at a very steep angle, as compared with its normal glide. With trailing edge brakes the technique is rather different; generally it is better to set the model up on the landing approach, enter a shallow dive towards the desired landing spot and then open the brakes to bleed off any excess speed.

Many modellers set their brakes or spoilers up on the fifth, or 'retract switch' function of their transmitter. I find this rather strange, since this then means that the brakes can only be either open or closed. Using the 'throttle' control on the transmitter to operate the brakes seems to be much more logical since they can then be used in a truly proportional sense, which can be very useful during descents from lift or tricky landing approaches.

To conclude this section, a brief word about flaps would be appropriate. Flaps differ from brakes in that, depending upon the angle at which they are deployed, they will produce extra lift, or a combination of extra lift and extra drag, or just extra drag. They can, therefore, be used in place of brakes when lowered to large angles (typically 70 degrees or more), but at the same time be used at small angles (5–10 degrees) to enable the model to be flown more slowly while searching for lift.

A further use of flaps, on a slope aerobatic model, is to couple them to the elevators so that, say, 40 degrees up elevator will give 20 degrees down flap and vice versa. These, operating in exactly the same way as a control-line stunt model's flaps, enable very tight manoeuvres to be performed.

With the use of modern radio, which permits the 'mixing' of various channels of control from the transmitter, and the switching in and out of such mixing at will, it is possible to produce all sorts of effects with flaps—coupling them to elevators for part of the time, then decoupling them for operation independently for both lift generation and braking. However, such advanced methods are really well outside the scope of this book and are only mentioned to give an indication of just what *is* possible.

Chapter 11
Power assisted soaring

IF CIRCUMSTANCES permit, the addition of a small diesel or glowplug motor to a simple slope model can produce a useful power trainer. However, one very important point needs to be made here; NEVER use the motor on a slope site, since such sites are almost always environmentally 'sensitive', and one transgression of this type may lead to the site being lost for all flying. Only fly the model on a field which you KNOW is approved for power flying.

While a small (say 50 inch) slope trainer with a .09 glow motor makes a satisfactory power trainer, much larger sailplanes can use the same size motor to produce a 'self-launching' thermal soarer, a type which can give much valuable thermal soaring practice with minimum fuss. Once again though; NOT, please, on a field which is designated for glider use only—many club thermal soaring sites are in noise-sensitive areas, close to houses, and can easily be lost by the thoughtless action of just one modeller.

The fitting of a motor to an existing design could hardly be easier. If the conversion is to be a permanent one, then the motor can be fitted in the nose of the model. Indeed, some enthusiasts have models with two fuselages—one glider, one power—and this is an economical way of achieving maximum flying time from your building investment.

However, if a removable conversion is the aim, so that the model can be used for occasional outings to the power field in between its principal role as a slope or thermal glider, then it is best to fit the motor on a pylon mounted power pod. Figs. 11.1 and 11.2 illustrate the principle of this, while Figs. 11.3 and 11.4 show some details of how a simple pod may be produced. In practice, such a pod adds surprisingly little to the drag of a large glider, and the soaring performance is little impaired.

If you are fitting a power pod to your model, please do not overpower it. Soaring sailplanes are very efficient

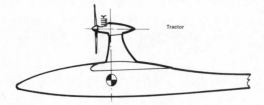

Fig. 11.1 Power pod—Basic concept.

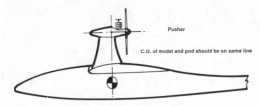

Fig. 11.2 Pusher.

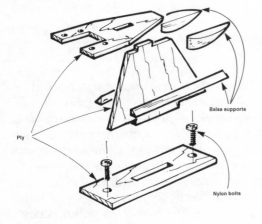

Fig. 11.3 'Basic' bolt on pod.

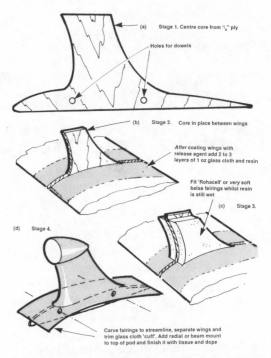

(a)   Stage 1. Centre core from ¼" ply

Holes for dowels

(b)   Stage 2.   Core in place between wings

After coating wings with release agent add 2 to 3 layers of 1 oz glass cloth and resin

Fit 'Rohacell' or *very* soft balsa fairings whilst resin is still wet

(c)   Stage 3.

(d)   Stage 4.

Carve fairings to streamline, separate wings and trim glass cloth 'cuff'. Add radial or beam mount to top of pod and finish it with tissue and dope

Fig. 11.4 More refined pod for plug together wings.

for a future book in this Argus series, but suffice it to say here that, while this approach is attractive, there are problems.

Electric flight is not entirely silent, models, and generally require very little power to climb away happily—the largest 10 to 12 foot open models will perform very adequately with a .09 glowplug or 1.5 cc diesel engine; fitting a bigger engine will only result in an overweight, overpowered combination. The model will be made to fly too fast under power, generating excessive lift, and such a model is neither comfortable nor safe to fly.

The other, at the moment, growing 'powered glider' field is that of electric flight. No doubt the whole area of 'electrics' will form the subject matter

Power pods for use in converting slope or thermal gliders into 'self-launching' models.

there is still the question of propeller and mechanical noise, but it is (at least in the form of self-launching sailplanes) sufficiently quiet to be acceptable on many thermal soaring sites. However, unlike the use of a power pod, there is a great deal of technical knowledge to be acquired if the installation and handling of an electric system is to be consistently successful. Also, a considerable payload of motor and batteries have to be carried (as much as 1.5 pounds for a relatively simple system), which means that the resulting model will be fairly heavily loaded. This in turn implies skilled handling. It would seem sensible to leave the application of electrics to your soaring model until a good deal of flying and constructional experience has been obtained, so that light yet strong structures can be confidently created and heavily loaded models adequately handled.

If, once experienced, the newcomer's thoughts turn to contest flying, he may well find electric soaring to be a fruitful field for experiment. It is only this year (1989) that 'electro-slot' soaring contests have started to appear on the competition scene, and with so few experts in the field, it is still wide open for newcomers to make an impact. The best approach to the contest class, both from the point of view of aerodynamic design, motor and battery systems and flying tactics has yet to emerge, so there is ample room for experiment and new thinking.

Conclusion

DUE TO THE format limitations of this particular series of books, it has only been possible to touch lightly upon many aspects of the radio control soaring hobby (or 'sport' as some people prefer to call it).

Once the newcomer has mastered the basic techniques of constructing models and flying them, the direction in which his interests develop is entirely up to the individual. Many modellers gain great satisfaction from just one or two models, which serve them through years of regular Sunday outings to the slope or field. This is fine, and is their way of enjoying themselves. Others have vast stables of aircraft, and are constantly building something new or seeking new challenges. This too is fine.

Many soaring enthusiasts never take part in a contest, while others do little flying except during competition. It all depends upon the individual. Even if contest flying is to be no part of your interests, it is well worthwhile to attend a few events in your particular speciality—slope aerobatics scale, thermal soaring, cross-country or whatever—just to spectate and see how others do.

Soaring is predominantly a business of skill and experience; it is just not possible to 'buy' success. Certainly good equipment makes life easier, but there is nothing required for most of the contest classes flown in this country which is not freely obtainable from the average model shop at prices which the average modeller can afford—except talent! The exception to this statement is, perhaps, the two World Championship classes of multi-task (F3B) and electric task (F3E) soaring. Here, if success is to be obtained at the highest —international—level, expenditure of money on relatively complicated radio equipment and support gear such as winches is going to be required.

In the meantime—just go out, fly on your hill or field, fly safely, with consideration for others, both modellers and general public, and enjoy one of the most creatively satisfying hobbies in the world.

Subscribe now...

here's 3 good reasons why!

Within each issue these three informative magazines provide the expertise, and inspiration you need to keep abreast of developments in the exciting field of model aviation.

With regular new designs to build, practical features that take the mysteries out of construction, reports and detailed descriptions of the techniques and ideas of the pioneering aircraft modellers all over the world – they respresent three of the very best reasons for taking out a subscription. You need never miss a single issue or a single minute of aeromodelling pleasure again!

SUBSCRIPTION RATES

	U.K.	Europe	Middle East	Far East	Rest of World
RCM&E *Published monthly*	£16.80	£22.80	£23.00	£25.30	£23.40
Radio Modeller *Published monthly*	£16.80	£22.40	£22.60	£24.80	£23.00
Aeromodeller *Published monthly*	£23.40	£28.20	£28.40	£30.20	£28.70

Airmail Rates on Request

Your remittance with delivery details should be sent to:

The Subscriptions Manager (CG/33)
Argus Specialist Publications
Argus House
Boundary Way
Hemel Hempstead
Herts
HP2 7ST